WAR AND THE POET

War and the Poet

AN ANTHOLOGY OF POETRY
EXPRESSING MAN'S ATTITUDES TO WAR
FROM
ANCIENT TIMES TO THE PRESENT

Edited by

Richard Eberhart
LT. COMDR., U.S.N.R.

and

Selden Rodman
M/SGT., A.U.S.

GREENWOOD PRESS, PUBLISHERS
WESTPORT, CONNECTICUT

Library of Congress Cataloging in Publication Data

Eberhart, Richard, 1904-   ed.
    War and the poet.

    Reprint of the ed. published by Devin-Adair, New York.
    1. War poetry. I. Rodman, Selden, 1909-   joint
ed. II. Title.
PN6110.W28E3 1974   808.81'9'3   73-19574
ISBN 0-8371-7287-X

DESIGNED BY PETER DÖBLIN

Originally published in 1945 by The Devin-Adair Company,
New York

Reprinted with the permission of The Devin-Adair Co.

Reprinted in 1974 by Greenwood Press,
a division of Williamhouse-Regency Inc.

Library of Congress Catalogue Card Number 73-19574

ISBN 0-8371-7287-X

Printed in the United States of America

PREFACE: ATTITUDES TO WAR

WAR poetry must be judged, like any other type of poetry, upon its essential excellence. The fact that men have written in all ages on war is as natural as that they have written on love, or on death. A time of war makes a survey of work in the field timely, within limits constricted by exigencies of the conflict. The implement of selection is, of course, taste, which in dual editorship must be synthetic. The scope of a war book, being arbitrary, could be any range of view, as large, or representative, or highly selective, or given to some critical bent, but in any case a selection of war poems cannot without immodesty, or even a raucous shout, be considered definitive. Taste will change. Time will further define.

From the welter of work examined since 1942, the present collection has taken its balance and shape. Actually begun under the last category to represent a critical tendency, it has grown toward the representative under *a priori* specifications which include an allowance of some poems not excellent by the strictest standards, but which are easily readable. And rather than choose the improbable abstraction of "great" poems, it has seemed to consist with the engagement of discovery to trace various attitudes poets have had to war, from ancient times down to the present. The weighting must be laid fundamentally to the strictures of taste; the omissions to be perceived must be excused on the grounds of the largest scope; while the framework of the four sections is recognizable as a categorical device.

The book may give the reader a sense of the continuity of man's varying reactions to war through the centuries. I began collecting poems on war in 1942. Later Selden Rodman evinced interest in the project and entered it as co-editor in the summer of 1944. We immediately set up a system for judging poems. Copies of projected entries were passed bearing a mark of

[v]

each editor in a scale of zero to three. A poem had to achieve a dual addition of four to be admitted toward final acceptance. Certain reversals of judgment occurred in the course of time, alterations upward or downward, but these, although inevitable, were, in fact, few in number. The principle of dual editorship was that two heads are better than one. What a volume might sacrifice in height of taste of one editor would be made up by the breadth of view of two. The idea was to rule out infractions of temperament, and to obey the dictates of reason. Compromise should prevail where possible. Where impossible, as in the small, residual percentage of poems violently liked by one editor, but equally violently disapproved of by the other, a new engine of procedure was set in motion, so that, instead of casting out poems due to single judgment, all the small, residual percentage was entered, thus securing to the reader the breadth of view mentioned, rather than canting the volume onto the bias of one attitude or approach. The whole effort of selection was to be a triumph of reasonable judgment.

Several poems in the book are considered in the nature of discoveries, revivals, or reappraisals. To mention some of these, the piece by Ennius, translated by John Wight, is for the first time translated into English. There are new translations from the Greek, Latin, French, Russian and German. The ballad by Martin Parker (1600?-1656?) revives the most prolific "ballad-monger" of his time, a sometime tavern keeper, soldier-of-fortune, author of "A New Ballad of the Swinefaced Gentlewoman," dweller in the ambit of Taylor, the Water Poet, and one who got himself into trouble with the Long Parliament of 1640. Boker's poem, considered as a discovery in 1942, has since been published elsewhere, reestablishing the Philadelphia poet and playwright. The contemporary reappraisal of Melville is continued. Cummings becomes one of the best war poets of World War I. Wolker and Halas have not been sufficiently read here.

Note should be taken of Friederich Adolf Axel Detlev von

Liliencron (1844-1909). He is the only poet in the book who boasts of loving war. He "wrote in 1889, at the age of 45, that he would give the whole batch of his writings for one day on the battlefield with his comrades-at-arms." Liliencron began writing at 35, "by accident." At 21 he was a Lieutenant in the Prussian army. He fought the French in 1870-71, was wounded in two battles. He came to New York in 1875, worked his way to the mid-West and Texas, returned to New York to play in a Bowery tavern. He was a symbol of the poverty-stricken poet living on the revolution of the word. His attitude may be seen in these lines: "Frei will ich sein, Freiheit der Kunst! Freiheit der Kunst vor allen! Frei sie sie Wie der Cowboy im Far-West."

The realism of his war poetry is seen in the passage where, fallen to earth, a horse is about to paw him. "I see the gash in the forefeet, / Blood running tear of the spurs, / The girth, the spattered coat, / The greatly swollen nut brown red belly." We are indebted to Gretchen Butcher for translation of this passage, as well as for the following lines, which also show Liliencron's realism:

Almighty God!
There lay my friend, torn and wide open
In the Sun's fire which soaked him up,
Still conscious of himself, yet beyond help.
His guts and entrails lay outside,
He stared at me in dying grief.

Hardly a week, and I'll be forgotten by the world,
Will be a table d'hôte, on which the worms will feast.

Selections of war poets of this century, or who have died in this century, are necessarily arbitrary. The interminable writings of Péguy, in his repetitive and clamorous search for religious truth, include the piece we have chosen as a war poem. Its meditative and elegiac nature allies it with his many litanies which sprang as if spontaneously from him, never being subjected to revision in the belief that they were dictated by the spirit. Péguy was killed on the Marne, September 5, 1914.

Apollinaire was more properly a war poet, entering the First World War in 1914. "Il en revint trépané en 1916." He died on November 10, 1918, "emporté par la grippe espagnole." A violent innovator, his poems have remarkable freshness today, although, unlike Péguy, his works have not enjoyed recent translation into English. Service men of the present, called upon to move from one island battle to the next, may be in the predicament of Apollinaire's "Class 'Sixteen," in his poem "Exercise:"

> Toward a village behind the lines
> Were going off four bomb-throwers
> They were covered with dust
> From head to foot
>
> They were looking at the vast plain
> While talking among themselves of the past
> And they hardly turned around
> When a shell had coughed
>
> All four of the "Class 'Sixteen"
> Were speaking of other days not of the future.
> Thus prolonged itself the asceticism
> Which was training them to die.

Yeats is anything but chiefly a war poet, yet his Airman's predicament was in a sense an ancient one, partaking of the tradition of the mercenary. The poem has been examined elsewhere and needs no comment here. The ill fate of Péguy and Apollinaire also befell Rosenberg and Owen. The fame of the latter has steadily mounted, while Rosenberg's "Collected Works" appeared as late as 1937. His "Poems," however, came out in 1922. It is only in the light of years that Rosenberg has come to be realized as one of the best of the World War I poets, far out-shining numerous poets celebrated at the time.

[viii]

Such a history must give editors pause in their selections of the poets of this war. It is conceivable that those now considered excellent will suffer a diminution of their excellence in the perspective of the future, while writers either little recorded and regarded now, or not known at all, may duplicate a career like Rosenberg's.

I have said elsewhere that the best war poetry achieves a universality of utterance transcending the particular: the best war poems are about Man. They express the poet's attitude to something beyond the immediacy of war, they comprehend a variety of interpenetrating meanings. It may be of interest to select certain poems not written by poets engaged in war as examples of non-participation provoking the greatest realizations, of excellence transcending the particular. Poetry being a complicated art, some of the examples in some ways contradict the thesis, and may live best in their particularities. Shakespeare evoked the vasty fields of France without going thither and our amusement at the sea-coast of Bohemia does not render the erroneous assumption less viable. Kant is said never to have traveled farther than thirty miles from Königsberg to embrace the meaning of the world; by the same token some of the best war poems have been written by poets the most reclusive.

Who would have thought of Emily Dickinson as a war poet? She was an intimate student of the murderous qualities of insects and birds in her Amherst garden, but one would hardly have expected her to have dealt with the problems of war. She exemplifies the power of the imagination to comprehend and control any elected meaning. In her three-stanza poem "Success is counted sweetest" she perceives that that is true "By those who ne'er succeed." The humanist tradition is maintained in the compact and incisive stanzas which follow:

> Not one of all the purple host
> Who took the flag today
> Can tell the definition,
> So clear, of victory,

> As he, defeated, dying,
> On whose forbidden ear
> The distant strains of triumph
> Break, agonized and clear.

The individualist's point of view is also expressed in "My Triumph Lasted Till the Drums," anticipating an attitude found in so recent a poem as "In Distrust of Merits."

Hardy saw "the mournful many-sidedness of things," as he said in "The Sick Battle-God." The poem "Channel Firing" is not listed in his Collected Works with the eleven poems designated as War Poems. Perhaps the best known of these is "Drummer Hodge." It is an honest poem and never falls into the meretriciousness which Housman sometimes and Kipling almost never escaped. "Channel Firing" is a war poem of a sort, obliquely so, based on "gunnery practice out at sea." It transcends the particular and looks to the Judgment Day with adequate Hardean irony and detachment. Indeed, this is a poem in which the transcendency of the particular is actually only another particularity. His sceptical intimacy in the manner in which God is made to talk is in contrast to the attitude, intimate in quite another way, assumed by Hopkins for the words of "Christ our King" in "The Soldier." Hardy's poem concludes with a root humanity of expression, entirely disinterested and natural, before the final quatrain, which in its last two lines flows with an enchanting music as delicate and subtle in movement as anything in his works, uncharacteristic only in that it is so much less rugged than most of his rhythms.

Hopkins was not at all a war-like man, yet in his time he was impelled to compose "The Soldier," removing the fact of "seeing of a soldier" to the universal considerations of "Christ our King." He was also intrigued by "A bugler boy from barrack," in "The Bugler's First Communion," which shows the same dual preoccupation with the flesh and the Godhead:

[x]

Here he knelt then in regimental red.
Forth Christ from cupboard fetched, how fain I of feet
  To his youngster take his treat!
Low-latched in leaf-light housel his too huge godhead.

And it may not be unallowed to speculate whether, had Hopkins lived at the present time, "Felix Randal" might not have been instead a poem to an F6F pilot or a B-29 gunner.

"The Soldier," then, could be written in 1885, without title, by a poet who could only be thought of as a soldier in the sense that he was a Jesuit serving Christ. Yet he perceived an immanence in the soldier, the immanence of Christ. Conversely, he perceived the manlikeness of Christ, revealed as Who "of all can handle a rope best." The speaking of Christ in homely terms was an attitude deeply ingrained in one who demanded the utmost concretion of image, the earthiest feeling, to bring abstraction into a muscular focus. Of all the war poems in the present volume, none is quite like this. Inimitable in style, it reaches deeply into the abyss of absolute meaning through the seemingly intractable originality of the diction which, once winnowed, as in all his works, gives increasing delight. The poem may be used as an example in an argument that a poet removed from actual war may actually perceive and transmit the meaning of war more pointedly than poets at war who are limited to present dimensions, present objectives and objects, immersed in the destructive element.

Frost, who is not alone in this, is a one-war-poem poet. As in all of the poets here under consideration, it might seem unlikely that he should write on war, yet it is so natural a subject, as we have said, that we discover his poem "A Soldier" without surprise. It was published in 1928. The compulsion would not seem to have been immediate, but the consideration verges on the universal. The universal in Frost is approachable, as in Hardy, from a less complicated position, and with less passion than in Hopkins or in Eliot. Frost's poem is neatly worked, he allows that the spirit of the fallen soldier "shot on," but he does not go very far beyond that. In fact, the last line retreats rather than advances in its modification, bringing into sharp focus the limit of Frost's imagination. He has consciously constricted his glimpse of the universality of the meaning into the safe limits of reasonable doubt.

Eliot's "Triumphal March," from "Coriolan," a poem written in his middle period, between the wars, is in every sense a war poem, although, again, Eliot is not strictly considered as a war poet, and has been silent with respect to the present war. As the profoundest of living poets, it remains to see whether he will speak specifically on this war. "The Waste Land" was obliquely a war poem in that it came out of the first World War, embodying the condemnation of a whole civilization, which condemnation, it is presumed, would not have occurred anterior to that cataclysm. "Ash Wednesday" and the religious plays engaged Eliot's release from the feelings of the post-war period, while the "Four Quartets" have proffered his late strict lyrical statements which, as in "And the fire and the rose are one," from "Little Gidding," hark back to and assimilate the essence "At the still point of the turning world" of the poem in this volume.

"Triumphal March" is actually a post-war poem, the celebration, as of a Roman triumph, after the event. It has the synthetic virtues of the famous style, compilation of images, seeing the event from several points of view, running back and forth through time, evoking our response to the visual scene, the implied meaning, the unseen presences "hidden under the dove's wing." His own philosophy, in the passage from which that phrase is quoted, is characteristically construed, or rather construed upon "The natural wakeful life of our Ego is a perceiving," quoted, as in his earlier method, directly from another writer, but without quotation marks, in this case from the philosopher Husserl.

The mid-catalogue of war implements already looks small compared with logistical figures predominating in World War

II, lending an archaic feeling in the reading not felt in the 'thirties. There is a suggestion of the Dictator, amorphous but massive, the leader. The subtle, shifting music of the verse gives on to the also characteristic parenthetical remarks about Cyril and the crumpets, which exercised so considerable an amount of prognosis and elucidation from London to Cambridge, Massachusetts. The poem concludes with a cryptic line, concluding the strategy of involvement of the whole context in a nexus of ramifying meanings.

There are so many poets in the fourth section of the volume who fall into the category of reclusive or unwarlike poets that we may well comment upon several.

Wallace Stevens' poem No. VII from "Esthétique du Mal" does not compare, in universality of utterance, with the poems of Dickinson, Hopkins, Hardy and Eliot. It is "the soldier of time" he is speaking of, "the wounds of all / The soldiers that have fallen, red in blood" which concern him. It is a poem stating the complex relationships of death-in-life, life-in-death. Even the soldier's wound is good because of life. "No part of him was ever part of death." The poem breathes a heavy, quiet, measured music, like a reverie of the mind in stately motion. If Stevens had left Hartford for a battlefield, he might have done worse, and it is idle to speculate whether he would have done better. He is not here dressed in the attractive motley he is used to wear. The meaning has dictated the sincerity, as it did to Marianne Moore when she abandoned her complacencies of the peignoir to write "In Distrust of Merits." She is a war poet principally in the one war poem included, in which she evaluates a personal moral dimension, actually an attitude of guilt. The bloodshed of which she writes has caused her to break through the decorative surface of her verse to the different kind of utterance in this poem. The feeling was in E. Dickinson, too.

Aiken, like Stevens, has sat out the present war, but unlike him has not been moved to long prose lucubrations on the subject. His poem "The Soldier" gives the feeling of the library rather than of the forward area. He has attempted an historical view of war through the ages, a compressed expression in miniature, analogous in another way to the perspective attempted in this anthology.

Edith Sitwell has changed in many poems, not one; there is currently a late period of her verse. Also uninvolved in war, technically, except insofar as everybody in England was involved in the war, she calls upon the Lord in "Still Falls the Rain," seeing our times inextricably bound to the days of the Cross and all our years inseparable as "the nineteen hundred and forty nails of the Cross." Her attitude is more conventional than Hopkins's and less odd than Hardy's. She yet employs the Eliot style, after twenty years, of admitting lines from other poets, as in the rolling, resounding Marlowan line included. She talks about Man, transcending the particular.

Auden, for the most part a non-participator in the war, and certainly an unwarlike man, said cogent things about war in the sonnet sequence "In Time of War" from his travel book "Journey to a War" written with Isherwood upon their journey to the East in 1938.

Prophetic now seem the lines:

> But ideas can be true although men die,
> And we can watch a thousand faces
> Made active by one lie:
>
> And maps can really point to places
> Where life is evil now:
> Nanking; Dachau.

"A bandage hides the face where each is living." "They carry terror with them like a purse." Many such statements make the sonnets as it were a set of introductory attitudes to the world-changing events which were to follow. It is only to be regretted that Auden has remained silent in later years, on the subject of war. He spoke that "Only happiness is shared, / And anger, and the idea of love." And for him the issues of war were quixotic:

Far off, no matter what good they intended,
The armies waited for a verbal error
With all the instruments for causing pain:

And on the issues of their charm depended
A land laid waste, with all its young men slain,
The women weeping, and the towns in terror.

I have chosen a few examples to make the point that the writing of war poetry is not limited to the technical fighters. The universal is no respecter of circumstances and in art there is no evasion of reality. The spectator, the contemplator, the opposer of war have their hours with the enemy no less than uniformed combatants. George Barker and Robert Lowell, one a pacifist, the other a conscientious objector, one an Englishman, the other an American, are represented with certain of their attitudes in this volume. In the long run, it is only the excellence of a poem which will maintain it in time. It happens to be my own bias that the best war poems are not limited to war, but transcend it, giving onto the deepest speculations about Man.

RICHARD EBERHART

INTRODUCTION: THE VISION OF ARMIES

PRIMITIVE peoples wrote poems to celebrate victories. The great epics were always war poems. Long before the Odyssey and the Vedic hymns an impressive poem was written about the prowess of the Babylonian King Gilgamesh, and set in cuneiform script on twelve clay tablets. That was about 2000 B.C. Not long after came the Egyptian chants from which Thutmose's Hymn to Victory was taken, and the passages in Exodus and Samuel.

Beyond an admiration of valor and a lament for the fallen there is not much revealed in these earliest poems of attitudes to war, but in the *Iliad* the feelings of the Greek and Trojan warriors are clearly defined and there emerges the beginning of a pattern which will persist throughout antiquity to Roman times—and beyond. The Hellenic view of life is implicit in Hector's fatalistic dialogue with Andromache before he goes to his death. He knows he is a marked man, that the gods have willed Achilles' victory; and the shame of not living up to the tradition of glory conquers his premonitory vision of Andromache in chains. Sarpedon puts it more cynically to Glaukos when he says, in effect: If we were immortal we could escape, but since we are not and must die some time anyway, let it be said at least, 'These were not obscure men.' Achilles cuts short Lycaon's plea for life with an unanswerable argument: 'Patroclus, a better man than you, died yesterday; and I shall have to die myself—so why all this clamor about it?'

With the lyric poets of the Greek Anthology a new note is sounded. The free cities are in danger and the citizenry is called upon to die, if need be, for country. 'How can man die better,' the Spartan Tyrtaeus asks, 'freely spending life to save his sons?' And Callinus: 'For great and glorious is a man defending home and children and his wedded wife.' Simonides in his matchless epigrams immortalizing the Spartans who died

[xvii]

resisting the first Persian invasion at Plataea and Thermopylae assured Greece that 'for lamentation they had memory': their fame would never die.

Only when we come to the great dramatists of the Periclean age, however, do we find any realistic account of war, any differentiation between leaders and led, any reflection on war's causes and effects, any premonition that the serious war poetry of the world will be anti-war poetry. Aeschylus, himself a warrior, whose epitaph reminds the Medes of his courage and omits to mention his writings, calls the god of war a 'money-changer of dead bodies.' The choruses in the *Agamemnon* cry out against the folly of the Trojan war, recalling bitterly the ten years of fighting on the alien soil (and mud) in Asia Minor—

> Continuous drizzle from the sky, dews from the marshes,
> Rotting our clothes, filling our hair with lice

and all, they add, 'for some strange woman.' 'Why make a computation of the lost'? the veteran asks. Glory it may be called in the history books, but the soldier himself is not taken in, and the poet is at pains to remind his civilian audience that 'the anger of these slaughtered men may never sleep':

> Heavy is the murmur of an angry people
> Performing the purpose of a public curse.

With Euripides, Aeschylus' anger gives way to pity and nostalgia—

> Dead and gone are the Kings of Ilium
> A plague, a plague held Greece

and in Aristophanes to whipping satire. 'Where,' asks Lysistrata, 'are the sons we sent to your battle fields?' And she demands to know why men, who continue to involve the state in wars of conquest, should be permitted to continue ruling.

How different, how characteristically different, is the Roman attitude to war! Even in the golden age of Augustus, the overtones are civilized but tired. The bloody Caesarian wars—the first world wars in a sense—had taken their toll. From the North, as Vergil remarked, Germany was stirring and the 'savagery of bloody Mars' filled the whole globe:

> deny not that this young man at least shall be healer
> to our collapsed world. We have paid enough long since
> in our own
> blood for the sins and the treachery of Troy and
> Laomedon.

Horace, the worldly cynic, the urban poet with a suburban villa for weekending, recalls his own flight from battle at Philippi with what some of our own latter-day pundits would call irresponsible amusement. He threw away his shield to return to the fine wines of his cellar, and he doesn't regret it. To be sure (with an eye this time perhaps to the Emperor and his retinue of censors and spies):

> Pleasant and fitting it is to die for one's country.
> But death tracks down the man who flies away
>   Nor does it spare the hams and cowardly backs
>   Of youths unwarlike.

No such nod to officialdom will be found in the poets of succeeding generations. As early as Propertius cynicism emerges unalloyed. Why should he even *write* about wars? Callimachus did without them . . . Love and the intrigues of court life are the poet's concern:

> I should remember Caesar's affairs—for a background.

Related to these only by time are the transcriptions from Eastern poetry which round out Part I of this collection. The

colloquy on war which opens the *Bhagavad-Gita* begins with
what is possibly the first statement of the case for pacifism in
any language. King Arjuna's revulsion as he approaches the
enemy is nobly stated:

> What can we hope from
> This killing of kinsmen,
> What do I want with
> Victory, empire. . . . ?
> How could we dare spill
> The blood that unites us?
> . . . Now let them kill me,
> That will be better.

But the answer of the prophet is the answer of Indian religious
teaching, and inevitably prevails: 'Your words are wise, Ar-
juna,' Sri Krishna answers him, 'but your sorrow is for nothing.
The truly wise mourn neither for the living nor the dead.
Bodies are said to die, but that which possesses the body is
eternal. . . . Therefore you must fight.'

This other-worldliness and will-to-death of Arjuna and Sri
Krishna alike is at the opposite pole to the practical wisdom of
the Chinese, at least as enunciated by Confucius and by Li Po.
The soldier is shown by the latter at last in his most character-
istic occupation—thinking of home. 'The Long War' is perhaps
the first overtly anti-war poem in any language. The poet in-
sists upon the detail of war as it is. The landscape might be
Verdun or Stalingrad:

> vultures tear . . .
> the long bowels of the dead
> Hanging them on the twigs of lifeless trees . . .

and the generals, 'who led them on'?—'they have accomplished
nothing'!

Brothers will battle   to bloody end
and sisters' sons   their sib betray;
woe in the world   much wantonness;
axe-age sword age   sundered are shields;
wind-age, wolf-age   ere the world crumbles;
will the spear of no man   spare his brother.

Such is the mood of the Eddas and the other Skaldic war songs written between 700 and 1000 A.D., the literature to, which Richard Wagner, and after him the Nazis went, for inspiration or sanction, but also the literature on which our language was firmly built and to which, every generation or so, when the tongue is in danger of becoming enfeebled utterly, we repair for renewed strength:

They were laden with franklins   and lindenshields
with Westland spearshafts   and with Welsh broadswords.
The berserkers bellowed   as the battle opened,
the wolf-coats shrieked loud   and shook their weapons.

This is the heritage to which Anglo-American poets from Chaucer to Donne to Melville to Hopkins to Auden to Robert T. S. Lowell have returned periodically and which has kept the poetry alive. Latin is a dead language and by comparison the poets in the romantic (Latin) tongues have been the poorer. It shows in the war poetry. After the Song of Roland and the troubadours of Provence, French became elegant—too elegant to describe war; there was a dearth, a drought, until symbolism late in the Nineteenth Century wrought its particular miracle. Italian poets after Dante made no attempt to deal with war except in polite knightly fashion. From the time of 'The Cid' and 'La Aurocana' to Lorca and the poets of the Civil War, Spanish poetry similarly appears to have shunned the subject. The 'Luciad' was imitated but not rivaled.

It was, to be sure, a period of chivalric wars, with the emphasis on personal combat and conservation of manpower, and this is reflected in English poetry from Spenser to Love-lace. But there were no cloths of gold in Marlborough's campaigns nor in the bloody wars of the Spanish Succession, and the underlying reality was reflected all through this time at least in the Scotch and English ballads of the yeomen and mercenaries. Sir Philip Sidney said that 'Chevy Chase' moved his heart more than a trumpet; and Ben Jonson would rather have written the poem (he is reputed to have said) than all his works:

> Of fifteen hundred Englishmen
> Went home but fifty-three;
> The rest in Chevy Chase were slain
> Under the greenwoode tree.

From 'Harlowe' and 'Malden' and 'Lord Willoughby' to 'Johnny I Hardly Knew Ye' and 'The Deserter' in the Nineteenth Century, the ballad never lost its edge. Burns built on it and Scott and Coleridge domesticated it, but its current continued, albeit sometimes underground. Peacock's satirical 'Dinas Vawr' saw it in a new incarnation and Southey's 'Blenheim,' that memorable epigraph to war like a toad in the Romantic garden:

> They say it was a shocking sight
> After the field was won;
> For many thousand bodies here
> Lay rotting in the sun:
> But things like that, you know, must be
> After a famous victory.

The American Civil War, perhaps because it was the first war to be fought by masses of conscripted citizens on both sides, and because it was by far the most lethal conflict up to that time, was memorialized by three poets unique in their treatment of the subject. Herman Melville was perhaps the first poet to be impressed by the innocence and lightheartedness

[xxii]

with which the youth go forth into the inferno. 'All wars,' he noted, 'are boyish and are fought by boys.' Stephen Crane who, although he did not actually go to war himself, wrote the first and in many respects still the most memorable, realistic war novel, in his single war poem told the mother contemplating the shroud of her son not to weep: 'War is kind.' But of the three the most revolutionary and one of the great war poets of all time was Whitman, who observed the fratricidal business from the vantage-point of what we would call today 'the medics.' It was the war, Whitman said later, that made him a poet and that generated his *Leaves of Grass*. In the section of that work entitled 'Drum Taps' he looks into the face of war from every perspective. He is not blind to the glory and the comradeship, but he refuses to soften the desolation and brutality. He tells a 'certain civilian' at the outset who might be looking for 'dulcet' responses

Go lull yourself with what you can understand, and with
    piano-tunes,
For I lull nobody, and you will never understand me.

Then he describes war, in 'The Wound-Dresser' and other poems like it:

I dress the perforated shoulder, the foot with the bullet-wound,
Cleanse the one with a gnawing and putrid gangrene, so
    sickening, so offensive,
While the attendant stands behind me holding the tray and
    pail.

But Whitman's reaction to war goes far deeper than the 'offensive' detail (which must nevertheless be included if the truth is to be approximated); he glimpses the ultimate tragedy in the death of the enemy—'a man divine as myself'—and finds (in the 'debris' of dead soldiers) consolation only in the thought that 'the living remained and suffered.'

Only Thomas Hardy, in the fastness of his Victorian study,

and Arthur Rimbaud after adolescent exposure to some of the perverse sadism of barracks' life during the War of 1870, were able during the Nineteenth Century to write of war with a comparable originality. Hardy, in a dozen lyrics as well as in *The Dynasts* subjected war as an institution to an ironic scrutiny quite as fearless and perhaps more devastating than Whitman's compassion. War, in 'The Souls of the Slain' resolves itself into a question:

> The sinister spirit whispered 'It had to be,'
> To which the Spirit of Pity answered 'Why?'

Rimbaud brings into sharp contrast man's inhumanity and nature's serenity. He touches upon the religious sanctions of murder. He asks no solution and brings no resolution. Anarchy is loose upon the world and it is enough to call it by its name:

> Give over everything to vengeance, terrors, wars.
> Come, spirit, let us twist inside the wound. Begone,
> Republics of this world! To all you emperors,
> Regiments, peoples, colonists, we say: have done!

Thus Rimbaud—before he gave up poetry at the age of 19 and prepared, symbolically, to trade guns for slaves in Ethiopia. And, as the century of progress closed, the Russian symbolist Aleksandr Blok saw fit to warn the West not to spurn the 'squint-eyed Mongolian' of the steppes lest again he make a pact with the 'Hun' and deliver Western 'civilization' over to Eastern vengeance.

III.

The First World War was not something new under the sun in the quantitative sense only; it was new in the depth of its impact on the psyche of soldiers and non-combatants alike; and consequently, once the character of that impact could be grasped by the mind, the source of a new poetic idiom was found.

Ruskin prophesied an aspect of this newness when he objected to modern wars on the ground that instead of being fought by those whose interests were at stake, they were fought by the common men into whose hearts mutual hatred had been poured by propaganda and who fought for national prestige and power of no value to themselves. Nevertheless the poets who set the key for the opening movement in 1914 were conscious of no such break with the past. It was enough to tell the young recruits in London that "Britons never shall be slaves." Kipling, the laureate of Empire and of the Boer War, wrote some enormously popular stanzas for the occasion:

> For all we have and are,
> For all our children's fate,
> Stand up and meet the war.
> The Hun is at the gate.

The young Georgians, with less bombast, but as lightheartedly, pitched their tents across the Channel in a landscape still graced with grass and trees. Gibson and Graves, Aldington and Sassoon sounded at first an elegiac note. Rupert Brooke in his last weeks at Skyros wrote movingly of the privilege of making 'some corner of a foreign land . . . forever England' in a mood that was not to be recaptured. There was a note of foreboding when the young Canadian poet John McCrae warned

> If ye break faith with us who die
> We shall not sleep, though poppies grow
> In Flanders' fields . . .

—but only a note. It was possible for a Robert W. Service to make even such a theme as 'On the Wire' bathetic.

Long after the reality had made, for those inured to trench and gas, such attitudes obsolete, it was in fact possible for the American soldier to repeat this pattern. The *Stars and Stripes* anthology of soldier verse never rises above good-natured beef-

[xxv]

ing and an echo of Kipling bravado. Dad's letters, Reveille, the cootie, parlez-voo, beans, Home is where the pie is, are favorite themes.

> Oh a mistress fit for the soldier's love
> Is the graceful '75.

Mud is still a matter of humor: 'Who said sunny France?' And as for the cause and the cure:

> there's just one guy to blame
> . . . and Kaiser Bill's his name.

Yet this was the war that Ernest Hemingway twenty-five years later, and in an essay calling upon men of good will to take arms once more, was to call 'the most colossal, murderous, mismanaged butchery that has ever taken place on earth.' And, he added, 'any writer that said otherwise, lied.' Attempting to explain why the only true writing that came through in 1914-18 was in poetry, Hemingway speculated that 'poets are not arrested as quickly as prose writers would be if they wrote critically since the latters' meaning, if they are good writers, is too uncomfortably clear.' We can guess that the explanation goes deeper than that, but the fact that the poets stood alone for years to come persists.

In Carl Sandburg, the war began to find its spokesman—but not quite. 'I am the grass; I cover all' expressed the utter impersonality of death at Passchendaele, but Hardy could have written it. Sandburg's apostrophe to the spider in the rifle—'go on, you're doing good work'—bespoke the futility that was beginning to be felt; but sentimentally. The revolution was not yet.

It came with Owen and Rosenberg, with Apollinaire and Marinetti, with Cummings and Pound, with George and Yeats. And with it counterrevolution, though not yet distinguishable, was mixed. Its greatest spirits did not survive to indicate the

[xxvi]

direction of its maturity. The lesser ones lived too long, made protest a religion and became sterile; and many became fascists, or the darlings of fascism.

What Wilfred Owen might have accomplished had he lived is speculation as futile as that gyrating around the death of Keats. In both instances the achievement qualitatively was of the first order. *Strange Meeting* is not merely the greatest of war poems, it stands out in any representative modern collection. *Greater Love* is a supreme lyric quite apart from its subject. But Owen was much more than the author of a dozen superb poems. He was a man resolved to change the world. He had already, when struck down at the Sambre Canal in those last November days of 1918, launched a 'crusade' to inform coming generations. The 'undone years' were not for him to be forgotten. He would never have counted himself a member of any Lost Generation. His poems, like Hopkins', or Donne's, were consecrated to a cause:

> I mean the truth untold
> The pity of war, the pity war distilled.

He was prepared to dedicate himself to the unrealized truth behind the slogans that had summoned all this sacrifice:

> I would have poured my spirit without stint
> But not through wounds; not on the cess of war.

But before exploring the possible heavens of the future it was necessary to describe the landscape of hell. He had seen it, and he described it—supremely in *The Show*, perhaps, which closes, following the desolation and the loneliness and the fear, on the most terrifying and exact of all war images.

If the other characteristic poets of World War I failed to achieve as universal an orchestration, each of them in his particular way fixed an aspect of the tragedy. Rosenberg, so close in spirit and language to Owen, achieved a poignant music and foreshadowed the rootless internationalism that was to flourish (ironically!) with most spasmodic intensity in Weimar Germany:

> Droll rat, they would shoot you if they knew
> Your cosmopolitan sympathies.

Sassoon brought out, too explicitly perhaps for poetry of the first order, the abyss between leaders and led, between the official idealism and the actual heartlessness. Cummings focussed most savagely the incomprehension of the homefront and the soldier's hatred for the civilian:

> a god damn lot of
> people don't and never
> never
> will know
> they don't want
> to
> no

Marinetti, the founder of Futurism, and Apollinaire, the father of Surrealism, sought method in the madness—the first by glorifying the destructive element, the latter by attempting to distill from the very efficiency and modernity of the cataclysm a residue of vigor, a purification, a depth:

> Before it we had only the surface
> Of the earth and of the seas
> After it we shall have the abysses

In all of these poets could be discerned the shape of what was to come, but in Yeats and Pound and Stefan George, an articulate prescience. Yeats' Irish Airman who acknowledges that he does not hate those he fights and that, beyond law and duty, he is caught up by a 'lonely impulse of delight,' is a symbolic figure. Pound, the only one of the three poets to become later an open advocate of fascism, indicts, in one of the most devastating of war poems, 'liars in public places' and the 'botched civilization' to which the soldier is about to return. But only George, German romantic that he was, diliberately set about creating a new mystique of militarism:

> We come to stand at our stern master's side
> We are happy reading from his eyes
> What shining dreams foretell us of our doom

Like his greater contemporary Rilke, George died in exile, but not before he had seen (uneasily) his innocent past contribute to the murderous future. What he had prophesied came to pass:

> All to which you grew through the glorious struggle
> Stays with you untouched, steels for future dins . . .

IV.

It was a tragedy for poetry as well as for Spain that Lorca, the symbolist whose roots went so deep that his poems were sung by the masses, should have been killed by the fascists in Seville before he wrote a war poem. For it was in that country, where the first battles of the Second World War were fought, that two styles in poetry, two attitudes to war, had a brief, unsatisfactory encounter. In the streets of Madrid, and at Guadalajara and on the Ebro, the poets of West and East compared notes. To Spain in those years came Ernst Toller and Ludwig Renn, Stephen Spender and W. H. Auden, Pablo Neruda and Michael Svetlov, André Malraux and Louis Aragon, Muriel Rukeyser and Ralph Bates. Had the International Brigades prevailed, an international style and an international war poetry might have been born. Neruda's savage indictment of the military and priestly instigators, his celebrations in controlled anger of the sacrifice, might have set in motion waves to break on every continent. As it was, the intellectuals and symbolists returned to their respective countries; disillusion

[xxix]

set in; the West appeased the common enemy and the East made a pact with him; and the way was prepared for the poetry of the war that followed to flow in two separate channels, as in fact it did.

In Soviet Russia the folk poetry of war that had begun to take shape out of the Spanish experience in such forms as Svetlov's 'Grenada,' burst forth in a national poetry of resistance to the invasion. Beginning in June of 1941 a total mobilization of the State's creative forces was decreed. Miraculously, we may think, the artists responded. Possibly never in the history of the world has poetry had such an audience. Volumes of verse and individual poems printed as broadsides were circulated by the millions. Some of the more popular poems were memorized and recited by whole armies. Chekhov's widow observed:

> 'We do not need poetry,' say the Germans, 'we need guns.' Well *we* need poetry. Our poetry is at the front. The genuine poet is aware today of one possible happiness—to live the lot of his country.

Four poets and three painters awarded the 100,000 ruble 'Stalin Prize' converted it into a tank whose adventures they then celebrated in song and canvas. Nicolai Tikhonov of the Writers' Union testified to the common feeling:

> The war, our motherland, love of freedom, revenge— these have begun to live in prose and in poetry. . . . If the fascists are impelled to glorify the slavery of all nations except the German, we shall write about the freedom of all nations; if they have debased woman to the lowest degree, we shall write verses and songs about the grandeur of our women, about youth, about beauty.

How good the poetry was by our standards it is impossible to say. Language and ideology are immediate barriers. Alexander Kaun who made a study of the new Soviet literature and who translated one of the poems included in this collection, assures us that the poetry was fresh, devoid of clichés, yet always understandable, and that along with the new came a great revival of the 'old' poetry. Among the new poets only Kirsanov retained traces of the Futurist formalism of Blok and Maiakovsky. Simonov and the other characteristic war poets wrote in terms of a simple dichotomy: tenderness for mother and child invoking implacable vengeance against their torturers; love of land contrasting sharply with hatred for its invader.

Jan Karski, in his *Story of a Secret State,* testifies to the same national revival of poetry among the hunted forces of the Polish underground:

> Never before the war did I understand what tremendous influence poetry may have upon a people fighting for an ideal. There was no underground paper which did not contain some poetry, verses of classic Polish authors or modern poets.

Similar revivals took place in France, and no doubt in the Balkan and Scandinavian countries too. But in France the folk poetry of the *maquis* and the urban underground had to compete with the new work of the most advanced poets in the symbolist tradition, and we begin to observe the cleavage between popular and sophisticated writing already noted. Two of the leading poets of pre-war Surrealism, Paul Eluard and Louis Aragon 'simplified' their own styles (not always happily) to meet the challenge. Other poets, refusing to compromise, continued to write in the oblique manner of the past.

In England and the United States where no vigorous strain of folk writing persists, an entirely different unfolding of war poetry came to pass. Its tone, if not its technique, may be said to have been established in the poems composed by the left-wing English school that dominated the new writing of the '30's—by Spender in Spain, by Auden during his visit to the front in China, by MacNeice during the first fiery months of the blitz in London. The political uncertainty and divided allegiances of these poets contributed to an aloofness, an elegant allusiveness, but also to an embracing nobility which was to be reflected in the younger and otherwise quite different poets who were to follow them.

This tone was reflected, too, in the new war poetry of several older poets who produced work of a startling freshness under the impact of the universal tragedy. Wallace Stevens, in a remarkable poem which evokes peace out of the timeless soldier's death, and Edith Sitwell in her passional elegy of the fire-bombing of London, could be cited. Marianne Moore's 'In Distrust of Merits,' a piece which has already been hailed by several poets as the outstanding war poem of the present war, wrung a lesson of personal humility out of the sacrifice of others. "They're fighting," she wrote, "that I may yet recover from the disease, *myself* . . . if these dyings can teach us how to live, 'these dyings were not wasted' . . . I must fight till I have conquered in myself what causes war." Compare this with Auden's much earlier invocation to the Chinese soldier who taught by his death

> that where are waters
> Mountains and houses, may be also men.

It is remarkable that none of the respected poets of England or the United States who took part in the fighting, or for that matter not one of the brilliant younger poets whose work began to appear during the war, wrote of war in their poems with any exultation. The kind of 'inspiration' and patriotic breast-beating that the Philistine critics had called for in their exhortations of 1939 never came. The puncturing of such moods which they accused Hemingway, Dos Passos and Cummings of having accomplished was indeed well done. The poets were not, as the Cassandras had feared, too disillusioned to fight, but they were too open-eyed by this time to write of the end except in terms of the means, and the means—they knew, even before stepping from the landing craft—was terrible. They remembered vividly what had happened to those poets of the last generation who had trumpeted the perfect peace (or the perfect state) sight unseen. MacLeish himself, in the more clairvoyant mood that preceded his denunciation of the "irresponsibles" had said it:

> Their bones were resultantly afterwards found
> under newspapers . . .

As it was, the transition in war poetry from the action level to the psychological that had been going on in the West for centuries, became complete. The aspect of war as a sport that had been legitimately celebrated by Shakespeare in Henry V's address to his troops at Agincourt was still an aspect, perhaps; but the modern poet would be inclined to leave its celebration to Hollywood. He was concerned with other truths, and his temperament was keyed to a darker penetration.

It was the sadness induced by watching a citizens' army in gestation that moved Harry Brown to perceive, 'a bond not of country, but of faith and love,' and Karl Shapiro to write 'Nostalgia,' that classic ballad of the soldier's aching bereavement on the troop transport. It was the irony of a private's decoration in a hospital ward that inspired Dunstan Thompson to ask:

> Who dares to say that love is like the war?

It was Roy Fuller's fierce resentment of the chaplain's clichés that made him cry out:

> O revolution in the whole
> Of human use of man and nature!

It was the clearsighted sensibility of a young pilot who died at the age of 21 to begin a poem as Rupert Brooke might have begun it with 'I burn for England with a living flame' and end it with the acceptance of death 'In a war for freedom who were never free.' Even the quasi-folk poetry of the Australian soldier, John Manifold, is informed with this vision of things, skeptical but not cynical, unillusioned but not disillusioned.

But as the war comes to an end another and a deeper note is heard, the reflection of a mood that is still too close upon us and too tentative to be more than touched upon here. To call it religious would be imprecise, but not entirely misleading. It is certainly such in the rock-like, violent images of Robert T. S. Lowell. It is equally present in the impassioned but motionless concentration of Demetrios Capetanakis who believed that suffering must be faced in all its 'nothingness' and 'ambiguity' but who nevertheless wrote before his untimely death in 1944: "No room in history is large enough to hold man's greatness . . ." It is perceptible negatively in Randall Jarrell's protest against the passivity of Marianne Moore's war poem: "Who is 'taught to live' by cruelty, suffering, stupidity, and that occupational disease of soldiers, death? The moral equivalent of war! Peace, our peace, is the moral equivalent of war." And it is present most triumphantly in Shapiro's sonnet sequence to the archtypical G.I. who dies without articulation or even consciousness of the ideals which are in the balance, but yet by the nakedness of his devotion to the group proving their possibility.

SELDEN RODMAN

CONTENTS

[xxxvi]

PART II

[xxxix]

[xl]

Part III

[xliii]

❧ *PART ONE* ❧

HYMN OF VICTORY: THUTMOSE III

Thou comest to me, thou exultest, seeing my beauty,
O my son, my avenger, Menkheperre, living forever.
I have given to thee might and victory against all countries.
I have set thy fame, even the fear of thee, in all lands,
Thy terror as far as the four pillars of heaven.
I have felled thine enemies beneath thy sandals.
My serpent diadem gives light to thy dominion.
There is no rebel of thine as far as the circuit of heaven;
They come, bearing tribute upon their backs,
Bowing down to thy majesty according to my command.
I have made powerless the invaders who came before thee;
Their hearts burned, their limbs trembled.

I have come, causing thee to smite the Eastern Land.
Thou hast trampled those who are in the districts of God's-
    land.
I have caused them to see thy majesty like a circling star,
When it scatters its flame in fire, and gives forth its dew.

I have come causing thee to smite the Western Land,
Keftyew and Cyprus are in terror.
I have caused them to see thy majesty as a young bull,
Firm of heart, ready-horned, irresistible.

I have come, causing thee to smite those who are in the
        marshes,
The lands of Mitanni tremble under fear of thee.
I have caused them to see thy majesty as a crocodile,
Lord of fear in the water, unapproachable.

[3]

I have come, causing thee to smite those who are in the isles;
Those who are in the midst of the Great Green hear thy roar-
ings.
I have caused them to see thy majesty as an avenger
Who rises upon the back of his slain victim.

I have come, causing thee to smite the Libyans,
The isles of Utenyew are subject to the might of thy prowess,
I have caused them to see thy majesty as a fierce-eyed lion
That maketh them corpses in their valleys.

I have come, causing thee to smite the uttermost ends of the
lands,
The circuit of the Great Circle is enclosed in thy grasp.
I have caused them to see thy majesty as a lord of the wing,
Who seizeth upon that which he seeth, as much as he desires.

I have come, causing thee to smite those who are in front of
their land,
Thou hast smitten the Sand-dwellers as living captives.
I have caused them to see thy majesty as a southern jackal,
Lord of running, stealthy-going, who roves the Two Lands.

I have come, causing thee to smite the Nubian Troglodytes,
As far as Shat they are in thy grasp.
I have caused them to see thy majesty as thy two brothers.
I have united their two arms for thee in victory.
Thy two sisters, I have set them as protectors behind thee.
The arms of my majesty are above, warding off evil.

I have caused thee to reign, my beloved son,
Horus, Mighty Bull, shining in Thebes,

[4]

Whom I have begotten, in uprightness of heart,
Thutmose, living forever.

AMON-RE, LORD OF THEBES
Translated by James Henry Breasted

THE LORD IS A MAN OF WAR

from EXODUS

THE Lord is a man of war:
The Lord is his name.
Pharaoh's chariots and his host hath he cast into the sea:
His chosen captains are also drowned in the Red Sea.
The depths have covered them:
They sank into the bottom as a stone.

Thy right hand, O Lord, is become glorious in power:
Thy right hand, O Lord, hath dashed in pieces the enemy.
And in the greatness of thine excellency thou hast overthrown
    them that rose up against thee:
Thou sentest forth thy wrath, which consumed them as
    stubble.
And with the blast of thy nostrils the waters were gathered
    together,
The floods stood upright as a heap,
And the depths were congealed in the heart of the sea.

The enemy said, "I will pursue, I will overtake, I will divide
    the spoil;

My lust shall be satisfied upon them;
I will draw my sword, my hand shall destroy them."
Thou didst blow with thy wind, the sea covered them:
They sank as lead in the mighty waters.

ANONYMOUS
King James Version

HOW ARE THE MIGHTY FALLEN

from 2 SAMUEL

THE beauty of Israel is slain upon thy high places: how are the mighty fallen!

Tell it not in Gath, publish it not in the streets of Askelon; lest the daughters of the Philistines rejoice, lest the daughters of the uncircumcised triumph.

Ye mountains of Gilboa, let there be no dew, neither let there be rain, upon you, nor fields of offerings: for there the shield of the mighty is vilely cast away, the shield of Saul, as though he had not been anointed with oil.

From the blood of the slain, from the fat of the mighty, the bow of Jonathan turned not back, and the sword of Saul returned not empty.

Saul and Jonathan were lovely and pleasant in their lives, and in their death they were not divided: they were swifter than eagles, they were stronger than lions.

Ye daughters of Israel, weep over Saul, who clothed you in scarlet, with other delights, who put on ornaments of gold upon your apparel.

How are the mighty fallen in the midst of the battle! O Jonathan, thou wast slain in thine high places.

I am distressed for thee, my brother Jonathan: very pleasant hast thou been unto me: thy love to me was wonderful, passing the love of women.

How are the mighty fallen, and the weapons of war perished!

ANONYMOUS
King James Version

HEKTOR TO ANDROMACHE

from THE ILIAD

ALL these things are in my mind also, lady; but I fear still
shame before the Trojans and the Trojan women with trailing
garments, lest like some coward I lurk far back from the fight-
    ing;
and the heart will not let me, now I have learned to be a brave
    man
always, and to keep fighting in the front rank of the Trojans,
piling high my father's glory and my own. For surely
I know this thing in my heart within and my mind knows it:
there will be a day at the last when sacred Ilion
shall perish, and Priam, and the people of Priam of the strong
    ash spear.

[7]

Still it is not so much the agony to come of the Trojans,
not even Hekabe and Priam our lord, that troubles me,
not my brothers who in their numbers and their high courage
must drop in the dust under the hands of these men who hate
   them,
as troubles me the thought of you, when some bronze armored
   Achaian
leads you off in tears taking away your day of liberty.
And you shall sit in Argos and weave at the loom of another
woman, and carry water from the spring Messeis or Hypereia,
sorrowful, but too strong will be the necessity upon you.
And some day far hence as he sees you in tears one shall say
   of you:
"This is the wife of Hektor, who fought always most bravely
of the Trojans, breakers of horses, when there was fighting at
   Ilion."
So shall they speak of you; but for you it will be only a fresh
   grief
to be widowed of such a man who could beat off the day of
   your slavery.
But may I be dead and the heaped earth huddled over me
before I hear your cries as they come to drag you captive.

HOMER
Translated by Richmond Lattimore

PATROCLUS' BODY SAVED

   from THE ILIAD

So THEY carried the dead man out of the fighting
With passionate effort towards the hollow ships.

But the fight dragged at them angrily, like a fire
That springs with a sudden leap on a human city
And flares till the houses vanish in a great light
When the hurricane's strength sets it roaring. So
Unintermitting, a clatter of horses
And of men with spears pressed on them as they moved.
They were like mules strung to the pitch of effort,
Who from a fell-side drag by a rocky track
House-rafter or big ship's timber, though sweat and fatigue
Wear down the courage in their tugging bodies.
With such effort they carried the dead man, while
Behind them the two Aiantës held the pressure
As a wooded spur holds back a head of water,
Sprawling across the lowland: even the dangerous
Torrent waters of strong rivers it holds;
Diverting instantly across the levels
Every current, it stands in the swirl unbroken.
So the Aiantës still held up the forward
Surge of the Trojans pressing close—in the van of them
Anchîses' son Aenêas and glittering Hector.
But the Greeks—as a cloud of daws or starlings passes
Screaming for life, the hawk once sighted,
To lesser birds a messenger of murder,
So before Aenêas and Hector the young
Men of Achaea rushed screaming for life,
Forgetting battle-gaiety: round the trench
Dropped from the runaway Danaans many a handsome
Piece of gear—and still no pause in the fighting.

HOMER
Translated by E. R. Dodds

[9]

SARPEDON TO GLAUKOS

from THE ILIAD

GLAUKOS, why is it you and I are honored beyond all men
with pride of place, the choice meats and the filled wine cups
in Lykia, and all men look toward us as if we were immortal,
and we are apportioned a great demesne by the banks of
      Xanthos,
good land, orchard ground and acres for the growing of wheat?
It is for us, therefore, in the foremost ranks of the Lykians
to stand firm and take our strokes from the blazing battle,
so that a man of our close-armored people may say of us:
"In truth, these are no obscure men who are lords of Lykia,
these kings of ours, who feed on the fat sheep appointed
and drink the exquisite sweet wine; but there is nobility
of strength in them, since they fight in the foremost ranks of
      the Lykians."
Man, suppose you and I escaping out of this battle
could be men who would live forever, ageless, immortal,
so should I not be myself a fighter in the foremost
neither urge you into the slaughter where men win glory.
But now, for the spirits of death stand ever around us
in their multitudes, no mortal can escape nor avoid them,
come, let us give some man his glory, or make it our own.

            HOMER
           Translated by Richmond Lattimore

ACHILLES TO LYCAON

from THE ILIAD

THUS spoke Priam's shining son with words supplicating
Achilleus, but the voice he heard again was pitiless:
"Poor fool, give over this argument and your talk of ransoms.
In time gone, before his death-day came to Patroklos,
always it was my heart's choice to be merciful
to the Trojans, and many I took alive and disposed of them.
Now there is not one man shall escape death, whom God only
lets me lay my hands upon before Ilion, not one
Trojan, and above all others not one of the children of Priam.
So, friend, you die also. Why all this clamor about it?
Patroklos also is dead, who was better by far than you are.
Look at me, what a man I am, how huge, how splendid,
begotten of a famous father and the mother who bore me was
        immortal;
yet for me likewise there is strong destiny and my own death,
and there shall be a dawn or an afternoon or a noon time
when some man in craft of war shall take my life also
by stroke of the spear cast or the arrow flown from the bow-
        string."
He spoke, and the man's knees went limp and his heart failed
        him.
He let go of the spear then and sank to the ground with both
        hands
extended. But Achilleus drawing his sharp sword
struck him in the neck beside the collar-bone, and the two-
        edged
blade cut clean within. He dropped to the dust face downward
and lay there prone, the soil drenched with his blood running.

HOMER

Translated by Richmond Lattimore

[11]

HOW CAN MAN DIE BETTER

Noble is he who falls in front of battle
  bravely fighting for his native land;
and wretchedest the man who begs, a recreant,
  citiless, from fertile acres fled.
Dear mother, ageing father, little children
  drift beside him, and his wedded wife;
unwelcome he shall be, wherever turning,
  press'd by want and hateful penury;
he shames his folk and cheats his glorious manhood;
  all disgrace attends him, all despite.
Come then,—if beggars go unheard, uncared for,
  spurn'd in life and in their children spurn'd—
with courage let us battle for our country,
  freely spending life to save our sons.
Young men, stand firm and fight, stand one by other;
  base retreat and rout let none begin.
Be high of heart, be strong in pride of combat;
  grapple, self-forgetting, man to man.
Forbear to fly, deserting men grown older—
  stiff about the knees, in honour old.
O foul reproach, when fallen with the foremost
  lies an elder, hindermost the young—
a man whose head is white, whose beard is hoary,
  breathing out his strong soul in the dust,
In nakedness his blood-wet members clutching—
  foul reproach, a sight no gods condone!
Naked he lies where youth were better lying—
  sweet-flowr'd youth, that nothing misbecomes.
Grown men regard the young, women desire them—
  fair in life, in noble death still fair.

Be steadfast then, be strong and firmly rooted,
  grip the ground astride, press teeth to lip.

TYRTAEUS
Translated by T. F. Higham

A CALL TO ACTION

How long, young men, unsoldiered, disregarding,
  laze you, scorned by neighbours round about,
Slack to the bone, on peace resolved, supinely
  careless in a land where all is war?

          .   .   .   .

  hurl in death your javelins once again.
For great and glorious is a man defending
  home and children and his wedded wife
against the enemy. At Fate's own moment
  snaps his thread of life. So forward all
with spear in poise, crouching to shields that cover
  hearts courageous, soon as battle's joined.
There's no escaping death: that destination
  men must face—ev'n of immortal seed.
Many from war and ringing lance have sheltered,
  homeward fled: at home death finds them out.
But these the people love not, none regrets them:
  brave men fallen great and small lament.
The whole land mourns a man of heart heroic
  dead: in life a demigod he seems.
His strength is as a tower to all beholders—
  work for many hands he does alone.

CALLINUS
Translated by T. F. Higham

[13]

AN ARMOURY

SPLENDID burns the huge house with bronze; rich is the ample
  roof
with radiant helmets; overhead each helmet lets a horsehair
  plume
droop, the warrior's ornament. Plates of armour hang on the
  pin,
greaves of radiant bronze, defence against the sturdy javelin.
Curved shields and cuirasses of new linen bestrew the room;
here are blades from Chalcis; here is many a cincture and kilt
  of proof.
These are things we must remember now our duty shall begin.

         ALCAEUS
       Translated by Gilbert Highet

ON THE LACEDAEMONIAN DEAD
AT PLATAEA

THESE set a crown of glory on their land,   1
 Death's livid mist compelled them, dark of death.
Dying they did not die. But out of Hades' hand,
 By the celebrant above, they are raised, Valor's breath.

         SIMONIDES
       Translated by R. E.

AT THERMOPYLAE

> TELL them in Lacedaemon, passer-by,
> That here obedient to their word we lie.
> > SIMONIDES
> > *Translated by various hands*

THE THERMOPYLAE ODE

FOR those who fell at Thermopylae
their fortune is blessed and their doom is splendor.
Their tomb is an altar, for lamentation they have memory,
    their pity is praise.
Such sacrament of the tomb
not rust nor time that beats down all shall make dark
for brave men. Their tomb has taken to itself to dwell there
the glory of Hellas. Witness Leonidas
king of Sparta, who left behind him the great
shining of courage, and fame that shall not die.
> > SIMONIDES
> > *Translated by Richmond Lattimore*

SALAMIS

Speech of the Messenger from THE PERSIANS

BUT when with her white horses day shone fair
And overspread the broad and ample earth,

There rose and rang from the Hellenic host
A roar of voices musical with psalms,
And loudly from the island precipices
Echo gave back an answering cheer. Thereat
Seeing their judgment grievously at fault,
Fear fell on the barbarians. Not for flight
Did the Hellenes then chant that inspiring hymn,
But resolutely going into battle,
Whereto the trumpet set all hearts on fire.
The word was given, and, instantaneously,
Oars smote the roaring waves in unison
And churned the foam up. Soon their whole fleet appeared;
The port division thrown out like a horn
In precise order; then the main of them
Put out against us. We could plainly hear
The thunder of their shouting as they came.
'Forth, sons of Hellas! free your land, and free
Your children and your wives, the native seats
Of gods your fathers worshipped and their graves.
This is a bout that hazards all ye have.'
And verily from us in the Persian tongue
There rose an answering roar; the long suspense
Was ended. In an instant, ship smote ship,
With thrust of armoured prow. The first to ram
Was a Greek; that impact carried clean away
A tall Phoenician's poop. Then all came on,
Each steering forthright for a ship of ours.
At first the encountering tide of Persians held;
But caught in the narrows, crowded without sea-room,
None could help other; nay, they fell aboard
Their own ships, crashing in with beak of bronze,
Till all their oars were smashed. But the Hellenes
Rowed round and round, and with sure seamanship

Struck where they chose. Many of ours capsized,
Until the very sea was hid from sight
Choked up with drifting wreckage and drowning men.
The beaches and low rocks were stacked with corpses:
The few barbarian vessels still afloat,
Fouling each other fled in headlong rout.
But they with broken oars and splintered spars
Beat us like tunnies or a draught of fish,
Yea, smote men's backs asunder; and all the while
Shrieking and wailing hushed the ocean surge,
Till night looked down and they were rapt away.
But, truly, if I should discourse the length
Of ten long days, I could not sum our woes.
There never yet 'twixt sunrise and sunset
Perished so vast a multitude of men.

AESCHYLUS
Translated by G. M. Cookson

"THE GOD OF WAR, MONEY CHANGER OF DEAD BODIES"

from AGAMEMNON

THE god of war, money changer of dead bodies,
held the balance of his spear in the fighting,
and from corpse-fires at Ilion
sent to their dearest the dust
heavy and bitter with tears shed,
packing smooth the urns with
ashes that once were a man.

[17]

They praise them through their tears, how this one
knew well the craft of battle, how another
went down splendid in the slaughter:
and all for some strange woman.
Thus they mutter in secrecy,
and the slow anger creeps below their grief
at Atreus' sons and their quarrels.
There by the walls of Ilion
the young men in their beauty keep
graves deep in the alien soil
they hated and they conquered.

The citizens speak: their voice is dull with hatred.
The curse of the people must be paid for.
There waits for me in the hooded night
terror of what may be told me.
The gods fail not to mark
those who have killed many.
The black furies stalking the man
fortunate beyond all right
wrench back again the set of his life
and drop him to darkness. There among
the ciphers there is no more comfort
in power. And the vaunt of high glory
is bitterness; for God's thunderbolts
crash on the towering mountains.
Let me attain no envied wealth,
let me not plunder cities,
neither be taken in turn and face
life in the power of another.

AESCHYLUS
Translated by Richmond Lattimore

[18]

"IF I WERE TO TELL OF OUR LABOURS, OUR HARD LODGING"

from AGAMEMNON

IF I were to tell of our labours, our hard lodging,
The sleeping on crowded decks, the scanty blankets,
Tossing and groaning, rations that never reached us—
And the land too gave matter for more disgust,
For our beds lay under the enemy's walls.
Continuous drizzle from the sky, dews from the marshes,
Rotting our clothes, filling our hair with lice.
And if one were to tell of the bird-destroying winter
Intolerable from the snows of Ida
Or of the heat when the sea slackens at noon
Waveless and dozing in a depressed calm—
But why make complaints? The weariness is over;
Over indeed for some who never again
Need even trouble to rise.
Why make a computation of the lost?
Why need the living sorrow for the spites of fortune?
I wish to say a long goodbye to disasters.
For us, the remnant of the troops of Argos,
The advantage remains, the pain can not outweigh it;
So we can make our boast to this sun's light,
Flying on words above the land and sea:
'Having taken Troy the Argive expedition
Has nailed up throughout Greece in every temple
These spoils, these ancient trophies.'
Those who hear such things must praise the city
And the generals. And the grace of God be honored
Which brought these things about. You have the whole story.

AESCHYLUS

Translated by Louis MacNeice

[19]

"THE ACHAIANS HAVE GOT TROY, UPON THIS VERY DAY"

from AGAMEMNON

THE Achaians have got Troy, upon this very day.
I think the city echoes with a clash of cries.
Pour vinegar and oil into the selfsame bowl
you cannot say they mix in friendship, but fight on.
Thus various sound the voices of the conquerors
and conquered, from the opposition of their fates.
Trojans are stooping now to gather in their arms
their dead, husbands and brothers; children lean to clasp
the aged who begot them, crying upon the death
of those most dear, from lips that never will be free.
The Achaians have their midnight work after the fighting
that sets them down to feed on all the city has,
ravenous, headlong, by no rank and file assigned,
but as each man has drawn his shaken lot by chance.
And in the Trojan houses that their spears have taken
they settle now, free of the open sky, the frosts
and dampness of the evening; without sentinels set
they sleep the sleep of happiness the whole night through.
And if they reverence the gods who hold the city
and all the holy temples of the captured land,
they, the despoilers, might not be despoiled in turn.
Let not their passion overwhelm them; let no lust
seize on these men to violate what they must not.
The run to safety and home is yet to make; they must turn
the pole and run the backstretch of the doubled course.
Yet, though the host come home without offence to high

gods, even so the anger of these slaughtered men
may never sleep.—Oh, let there be no fresh wrong done!

AESCHYLUS

Translated by Richmond Lattimore

THEBES OF THE SEVEN GATES

from ANTIGONE

CHORUS:

STROPHE 1

Now the long blade of the sun, lying
Level east to west, touches with glory
Thebes of the Seven Gates. Open, unlidded
Eye of golden day! O marching light
Across the eddy and rush of Dirce's stream,
Striking the white shields of the enemy
Thrown headlong back from the blaze of morning!

CHORAGOS:

Polyneices their commander
Roused them with windy phrases,
He the wild eagle screaming
Insults above our land,
His wings their shields of snow,
His crest their marshalled helms.

CHORUS:

ANTISTROPHE 1

Against our seven gates in a yawning ring
The famished spears came onward in the night;

[21]

But before his jaws were sated with our blood,
Or pinefire took the garland of our towers,
He was thrown back; and as he turned, great Thebes—
No tender victim for his noisy power—
Rose like a dragon behind him, shouting war.

CHORAGOS:

For God hates utterly
The bray of bragging tongues;
And when he beheld their smiling,
Their swagger of golden helms,
The frown of his thunder blasted
Their first man from our walls.

CHORUS:

STROPHE 2

We heard his shout of triumph high in the air
Turn to a scream; far out in a flaming arc
He fell with his windy torch, and the earth struck him.
And others storming in fury no less than his
Found shock of death in the dusty joy of battle.

CHORAGOS:

Seven captains at seven gates
Yielded their clanging arms to the god
That bends the battle-line and breaks it.
These two only, brothers in blood,
Face to face in matchless rage,
Mirroring each the other's death,
Clashed in long combat.

CHORUS:

ANTISTROPHE 2

But now in the beautiful morning of victory
Let Thebes of the many chariots sing for joy!

[22]

With hearts for dancing we'll take leave of war:
Our temples shall be sweet with hymns of praise,
And the long night shall echo with our chorus.

SOPHOCLES
Translated by Dudley Fitts
and Robert Fitzgerald

CHORUS: THE KINGS OF TROY

from ANDROMACHE

O PHOEBUS embattling the high wall of Ilium,
And thou of ocean, guiding behind black horses
    Thy chariot on salt water,
        Why have ye, in what wrath,
        Given the work of your hands—
        A fine work scorned, to the spear
    Of war, deserting unhappy
            Unhappy Troy?

Many on Símoïs banks were the quick chariots
Inspanned, and bloody the ungarlanded racing
    That ye for mortals made there:
        Dead and gone are the kings
        Of Ilium, and no fire
        On altar-hearth now burns,
    There is no more incense smoking
           In Troy for Gods.

Gone is the son of Atreus, wifely hands
Killed him, and she, requited by her children,
    Suffered God's anger, dying.

[23]

The word of God prophetic turned on her,
When, out of Argos, Agamemnon's son
Trod the rich temple floors and went to be
                 The killer of his mother.
         O God, can I trust thy word, O Phoebus?

Troy's women all through the Grecian market places
Sang lamentations for their unlucky children,
                 And wives must home abandon
To follow another man; it is not you
Alone on whom fell difficult grief, it is not
Your friends alone. A plague, a plague held Greece;
                 And to deep fields in Phrygia
Crossed over a storm, and rained down murder.

EURIPIDES
Translated by George Allen

THE AFTERMATH

from IPHIGENEIA IN AULIS

PERGAMON city of the Phrygians,
city of the stone towers, shall be
circled in blood and warfare.
Atreus' son shall drag away
Paris by the torn hair,
utterly sack the city,
leave in tears the daughters
of Troy and the queen of Priam.
Helen the god's child
sits weeping

her husband forsaken.
Never to me,
never to my children's children
let there come such expectation
as keep now the golden
Lydian women, these wives
of the Trojans, standing beside their looms,
whispering to each other:
"What man shall lay strong hands
on my hair in its glory,
to drag me weeping, reft of my perished country:
all for you, O child of the swan slim-throated,
if such a tale be true
how Zeus' shape changed as he came
to Leda, a bird winged,
even if the stories came down
in the folded books of the Muses
false before men and a vanity.

EURIPIDES
Translated by Richmond Lattimore

HOW THE WOMEN WILL STOP WAR

from LYSISTRATA

Magistrate. Lysistrata.

MAG. You, I presume, could adroitly and gingerly
      settle this intricate, tangled concern:
     You in a trice could relieve our perplexities.
LYS. Certainly.

[25]

MAG.	How? Permit me to learn.

LYS.   Just as a woman, with nimble dexterity,
        thus with her hands disentangles a skein,
    Hither and thither her spindles unravel it,
        drawing it out, and pulling it plain.
    So would this weary Hellenic entanglement
        soon be resolved by our womanly care,
    So would our embassies neatly unravel it,
        drawing it here and pulling it there.

MAG.   Wonderful, marvellous feats, not a doubt of it,
        you with your skeins and your spindles can show:
    Fools! do you really expect to unravel a
        terrible war like a bundle of tow?

LYS.   Ah, if you only could manage your politics
        just in the way that we deal with a fleece!

MAG.   Tell us the recipe.

LYS.   First, in the washing-tub
    plunge it, and scour it, and cleanse it from grease,
    Purging away all the filth and the nastiness;
        then on the table expand it and lay,
    Beating out all that is worthless and mischievous,
        picking the burrs and the thistles away.
    Next, for the clubs, the cabals, and the coteries,
        banding unrighteously, office to win,
    Treat them as clots in the wool, and dissever them,
        lopping the heads that are forming therein.
    Then you should card it, and comb it, and mingle it,
        all in one basket of love and of unity,
    Citizens, visitors, strangers, and sojourners,
        all the entire, undivided community.
    Know you a fellow in debt to the Treasury?
        Mingle him merrily in with the rest.

[26]

Also remember the cities, our colonies,
    outlying states in the east and the west,
Scattered about to a distance surrounding us,
    these are our shreds and our fragments of wool;
These to one mighty political aggregate
    tenderly, carefully, gather and pull,
Twining them all in one thread of good fellowship;
    thence a magnificent bobbin to spin,
Weaving a garment of comfort and dignity,
    worthily wrapping the People therein.

MAG. Heard any ever the like of their impudence,
    those who have nothing to do with the war,
Preaching of bobbins, and beatings, and washing-tubs?

LYS.   Nothing to do with it, wretch that you are!
We are the people who feel it the keenliest,
    doubly on us the affliction is cast;
Where are the sons that we sent to your battlefields?

MAG.   Silence! a truce to the ills that are past.

LYS. Then in the glory and grace of our womanhood,
    all in the may and the morning of life,
Lo, we are sitting forlorn and disconsolate,
    what has a soldier to do with a wife?
We might endure it, but ah! for the younger ones,
    still in their maiden apartments they stay,
Waiting the husband that never approaches them,
    watching the years that are gliding away.

MAG. Men, I suppose, have their youth everlastingly.

LYS.   Nay, but it isn't the same with a man:
Grey though he be when he comes from the battlefield,
    still if he wishes to marry, he can.
Brief is the spring and the flower of our womanhood,
    once let it slip, and it comes not again;

Sit as we may with our spells and our auguries,
never a husband will marry us then.

ARISTOPHANES
Translated by B. B. Rogers

EPIGRAM FOR THE DEAD AT TEGEA

IT WAS by these men's valor that wide-lawned Tegea never
burned and the smoke went never up into the bright sky.
So they wished it; to leave to their children a city shining
in liberty, and themselves to go down in the first wave.

ANONYMOUS
Translated by Richmond Lattimore

THE BATTLE

"WE GRASP our battle spears: we don our breast-plates of
hide.
The axles of our chariots touch: our short swords meet.
Standards obscure the sun: the foe roll up like clouds.
Arrows fall thick: the warriors press forward.
They menace our ranks: they break our line.
The left-hand trace-horse is dead: the one on the right is
smitten.
The fallen horses block our wheels: they impede the yoke-
horses!"

They grasp their jade drum-sticks: they beat the sounding
drums.
Heaven decrees their fall: the dread Powers are angry.

The warriors are all dead: they lie on the moor-field.
They issued but shall not enter: they went but shall not return.
The plains are flat and wide; the way home is long.
Their swords lie beside them: their black bows, in their hand.

Though their limbs be torn, their hearts could not be re-
pressed.
They were more than brave: they were inspired with the spirit
of "Wu."
Steadfast to the end, they could not be daunted.
Their bodies were stricken, but their souls have taken Immor-
tality—
Captains among the ghosts, heroes among the dead.

CHU YUAN
Translated by Arthur Waley

EPITAPH

Inscription from Anticyra

THEY whose life is given utterly over to valor,
these are the first to die in the shock and terror of war.

ANONYMOUS
Translated by Richmond Lattimore

"LIKE A SHOWER OF RAIN"

from the ANNALES

LIKE a shower of rain
The weapons on the tribune:

They pierce his shield.
The boss is ringing with spears;
From his helmet glances a shrill sound!

Not one of all the adversaries
Can cut down his body
With the gleaming sword.

Always he shatters or strikes
Down the abundant spears.
Sweat bathes his whole body;

He labors greatly
He cannot breathe.

ENNIUS
Translated by John Wight

FIGHTING SOUTH OF THE CASTLE

THEY fought south of the Castle,
They died north of the wall.
They died in the moors and were not buried.
Their flesh was the food of crows.

[30]

"Tell the crows we are not afraid;
We have died in the moors and cannot be buried.
Crows, how can our bodies escape you?"
The waters flowed deep
And the rushes in the pool were dark.
The riders fought and were slain:
Their horses wander neighing.
By the bridge there was a house.
Was it south, was it north?
The harvest was never gathered.
How can we give you your offerings?
You served your Prince faithfully,
Though all in vain.
I think of you, faithful soldiers;
Your service shall not be forgotten.
For in the morning you went out to battle
And at night you did not return.

ANONYMOUS
Translated by Arthur Waley

WE HAVE PAID ENOUGH
LONG SINCE IN OUR OWN BLOOD

from the GEORGICS

THEREFORE Philippi saw once more the Roman battalions
clash upon each other with weapons matched; and the high
    gods
deigned twice over that with our blood the wide fields of
    Haemus
and Emathia be made fat and flourish. Surely the time shall

come when in those reaches the farmer following the plow-
    share
cramped to earth shall come on javelins thin with the rust-rot
or with the weight of the mattock turn up hollow helmets.
Gods of our fathers grown to our soil, O Romulus, Vesta
mother and savior of Tuscany, Tiber, Rome's Palatine ridges,
deny not that this young man at least shall be healer
to our collapsed world. We have paid enough long since in our
    own
blood for the sins and the treachery of Troy and Laomedon.
Now long since the kingdom of the sky has envied you, Caesar,
us and you, is sick of bringing to pass the triumphs of mortals,
right sometimes and sometimes wicked; the world at warfare
so many times; so many faces of cruelty; never the farmer's
right he merits; the tillers swept away and the fields gone
foul, the curved reaping-hooks beaten stark into sword-blades.
From the east Euphrates, from the north Germany stirs to
    battle.
Close cities have broken their links of peace and go armed now
for civil strife; the savagery of bloody Mars fills the whole
    globe.
As when chariots for racing have burst from their caverned
stalls, go wild abroad, and with vain hands clutching the
    guide-reins
helpless the charioteer is carried at the will of his horses.

VERGIL

Translated by Richmond Lattimore

[32]

"RANG'D ON THE LINE OPPOSED, ANTONIUS BRINGS"

from the AENEID

Rang'd on the line oppos'd, Antonius brings
Barbarian aids, and troops of Eastern kings;
Th'Arabians near, the Bactrians from afar,
Of tongues discordant, and a mingled war:
And, rich in gaudy robes, amidst the strife,
His ill fate follows him—th' Egyptian wife.
Moving they fight; with oars and forky prows
The froth is gather'd, and the water glows.
It seems, as if the Cyclades again
Were rooted up, and justled in the main;
Or floating mountains floating mountains meet;
Such is the fierce encounter of the fleet.
Fireballs are thrown, and pointed jav'lins fly;
The fields of Neptune take a purple dye.
The queen herself, amidst the loud alarms,
With cymbals toss'd her fainting soldiers warms—
Fool as she was! who had not yet divin'd
Her cruel fate, nor saw the snakes behind.
Her country's gods, and monsters of the sky,
Great Neptune, Pallas, and Love's Queen defy:
The dog Anubis barks, but barks in vain,
No longer dares oppose th' ethereal train.
Mars in the middle of the shining shield
Is grav'd and strides along the liquid field.
The Diræ souse from heav'n with swift descent;
And Discord, dyed in blood, with garments rent,
Divides the prease: her steps Bellona treads,

[33]

And shakes her iron rod above their heads.
This seen, Apollo, from his Actian height,
Pours down his arrows; at whose winged flight
The trembling Indians and Egyptians yield,
And soft Sabæans quit the wat'ry field.
The fatal mistress hoists her silken sails,
And, shrinking from the fight, invokes the gales.
Aghast she looks, and heaves her breast for breath,
Panting, and pale with fear of future death.
The god had figur'd her as driv'n along
By winds and waves, and scudding thro' the throng.
Just opposite, sad Nilus opens wide
His arms and ample bosom to the tide,
And spreads his mantle o'er the winding coast,
In which he wraps his queen, and hides the flying host.
The victor to the gods his thanks express'd,
And Rome, triumphant, with his presence bless'd.
Three hundred temples in the town he plac'd;
With spoils and altars ev'ry temple grac'd.
Three shining nights, and three succeeding days,
The fields resound with shouts, the streets with praise,
The domes with songs, the theaters with plays.

VERGIL

Translated by John Dryden

ODES: II, 7

POMPEIUS, best of all my comrades, you and I
Often faced death when we were rebels.
Who brings you back, a citizen again,
To Italian gods and sky?

With ointment on our hair and wine
We helped along the days that used to linger.
We went through Philippi's swift rout together, too.
That little shield of mine

Was thrown away, while all around us
Courage broke and the threateners,
Chins in the dust, grovelled on
The disgraceful ground.

Me out of danger's reach the god of poets bore
Swiftly through the sustaining air;
You the boiling tides sucked back again
To fight once more.

Finally, your lengthy service ended,
Lay your weariness beneath my laurel tree.
Feast, and do not overlook the dreamy Massic
Just for you intended.

Fill up the polished cups. Whom will the Venus-throw receive
As drinking master? Who will see that crowns are made
Of parsley with the moisture still upon it
Or of myrtle leaves?

Pour ointment from the shells, and comb
It in your hair. I will drink like any toper.
For it is sweet to be a little mad
When a friend comes home.

HORACE
Translated by John Wight

[35]

Lᴇᴛ the youth hardened by a sharp soldier's life
Learn thoroughly to suffer cheerfully harsh injury, and
   Let him as a horseman feared because of his spear
      Harass the ferocious Parthians,

And let him lead his life under the open sky and among
Scenes of peril. As she watches him from hostile battlements,
   Let the warring tyrant's ripening daughter,
      Watched by her mother, yet sigh out,

"Alas, let not the royal bridegroom, unskilled
In conflicts, stir up the lion harsh to the touch,
   Whom bloody wrath snatches through
      The midst of slaughters."

Pleasant and fitting it is to die for one's own country.
But death tracks down the man who flies away,
   Nor does it spare the hams or cowardly backs
      Of youths unwarlike.

Martial courage, which knows nothing of disgraceful defeat,
Gleams with untarnishable honors; it neither
   Takes up nor lays down the axes
      At the breath of popular favor.

Laying open the heavens for those who do not deserve to die,
It forces its way by a course denied to common men
   And scorns with flying wing the mouldering earth
      And the common comings-together.

There is assured reward for faithful silence: I will forbid
Him who spreads to the multitude the sacred rites of mystic
    Ceres
  To be with me under these same beams, and to set sail
    His fragile skiff with me again.

Often the neglected Sky-Father involves
The unspotted with the defiled man. Rarely does retribution
  With halting steps abandon the wicked man,
    Even though he has the head start.
                 HORACE
             Translated by Gardner Taplin & R. E.

TURNING ASIDE FROM BATTLES

THUS much the fates have allotted me, and if, Maecenas,
I were able to lead heroes into armour, I would not,
Neither would I warble of Titans, nor of Ossa spiked onto
    Olympus,
Nor of causeways over Pelion,
Nor of Thebes in its ancient respectability, nor of Homer's
    reputation in Pergamus,
Nor of Xerxes' two-barreled kingdom, nor of Remus and his
    royal family,
Nor of dignified Carthaginian characters,
Nor of Welsh mines and the profit Marus had out of them.
I should remember Caesar's affairs . . . for a background,
Although Callimachus did without them, and without Theseus,
Without an inferno, without Achilles attended of gods,
Without Ixion, and without the sons of Menoetius and
    the Argo and without Jove's grave and the Titans.

And my ventricles do not palpitate to Caesarial *ore rotundos,*
Nor to the tune of the Phrygian fathers.

Sailor, of winds; a plowman, concerning his oxen;
Soldier, the enumeration of wounds; the sheep-feeder, of ewes;
We, in our narrow bed, turning aside from battles:
Each man where he can, wearing out the day in his manner.

SEXTUS PROPERTIUS
Ezra Pound's Version

DEBATE BETWEEN ARJUNA AND SRI KRISHNA

from the BHAGAVAD-GITA

ARJUNA:

KRISHNA, Krishna,
Now as I look on
These my kinsmen
Arrayed for battle,
My limbs are weakened,
My mouth is parching,
My body trembles,
My hair stands upright,
My skin seems burning,
The bow Gandiva
Slips from my hand,
My brain is whirling
Round and round,
I can stand no longer:

[38]

Krishna, I see such
Omens of evil!
What can we hope from
This killing of kinsmen,
What do I want with
Victory, empire,
Or their enjoyment?

*

Evil they may be,
Worst of the wicked,
Yet if we kill them
Our sin is greater.
How could we dare spill
The blood that unites us?
Where is joy in
The killing of kinsmen?

*

We know what fate falls
On families broken:
The rites are forgotten,
Vice rots the remnant
Defiling the women,
And from their corruption
Comes mixing of castes:
The curse of confusion
Degrades the victims
And damns the destroyers.
The rice and the water
No longer are offered;
The ancestors also
Must fall dishonored
From home in heaven.

[39]

Such is the crime
Of the killers of kinsmen:
The ancient, the sacred,
Is broken, forgotten.
Such is the doom
Of the lost, without caste-rites:
Darkness and doubting
And hell forever.

What is this crime
I am planning, O Krishna?
Murder most hateful,
Murder of brothers!
Am I indeed
So greedy for greatness?

Rather than this
Let the evil children
Of Dhritarashtra
Come with their weapons
Against me in battle:
I shall not struggle,
I shall not strike them.
Now let them kill me,
That will be better.

SRI KRISHNA:

Your words are wise, Arjuna, but your sorrow is for nothing.
The truly wise mourn neither for the living nor for the
dead.

[40]

There was never a time when I did not exist, nor you, nor any of these kings. Nor is there any future in which we shall cease to be.

Just as the dweller in this body passes through childhood, youth and old age, so at death he merely passes into another kind of body. The wise are not deceived by that.

Feelings of heat and cold, pleasure and pain, are caused by the contact of the senses with their objects. They come and they go, never lasting long. You must accept them.

A serene spirit accepts pleasure and pain with an even mind, and is unmoved by either. He alone is worthy of immortality.

That which is non-existent can never come into being, and that which is can never cease to be. Those who have known the inmost Reality know also the nature of *is* and *is not*.

That Reality which pervades the universe is indestructible. No one has power to change the Changeless.

Bodies are said to die, but That which possesses the body is eternal. It cannot be limited, or destroyed. Therefore you must fight.

*

Dream not you do
The deed of the killer,
Dream not the power

[41]

Is yours to command it.
Worn-out garments
Are shed by the body:
Worn-out bodies
Are shed by the dweller
Within the body.
New bodies are donned
By the dweller, like garments.

Not wounded by weapons,
Not burned by fire,
Not dried by the wind,
Not wetted by water:
Such is the Atman,

Not dried, not wetted,
Not burned, not wounded,
Innermost element,
Everywhere, always,
Being of beings,
Changeless, eternal,
For ever and ever.

*

ANONYMOUS
*Translated by Swami Prabhavananda
and Christopher Isherwood*

LAMENT OF THE FRONTIER GUARD

BY THE North Gate, the wind blows full of sand,
Lonely from the beginning of time until now!

Trees fall, the grass goes yellow with autumn.
I climb the towers and towers to watch out the barbarous land:
Desolate castle, the sky, the wide desert.
There is no wall left to this village.
Bones white with a thousand frosts,
High heaps, covered with trees and grass;
Who brought this to pass?
Who has brought the flaming imperial anger?
Who has brought the army with drums and with kettle-drums?
Barbarous kings.
A gracious spring, turned to blood-ravenous autumn,
A turmoil of wars-men, spread over the middle kingdom,
Three hundred and sixty thousand,
And sorrow, sorrow like rain.
Sorrow to go, and sorrow, sorrow returning.
Desolate, desolate fields,
And no children of warfare upon them,
No longer the men for offence and defence.
Ah, how shall you know the dreary sorrow at the North Gate,
With Li Po's name forgotten,
And we guardsmen fed to the tigers.

Li Po
Translated by Ezra Pound

THE LONG WAR

They fought last year by the upper valley of Son-Kan,
This year by the high ranges of the Leek Mountains,
They are still fighting . . . fighting! . . .
They wash their swords and armor in the cold waves of the
    Tiao-Chih Sea;

[43]

Their horses, turning loose over the Tien Mountains,
Seek the meagre grasses in the white snow.

Long, long have they been fighting, full ten thousand li away
    from home;
Their armor is worn out, the soldiers grown old. . . .

Oh, the warlike Tartars!
To them manslaughter is their plowing,
Plowing, oh from ancient times, in the fields of white bones
    and yellow sands!

It was in vain that the Emperor of Chin built the Great Wall,
Hoping to shut out those fiery hordes.
Where the wall stands, down to the Han Dynasty,
The beacon fires are still burning.

The beacon fires keep on burning;
The war will never cease! . . .

The soldiers fight and die in death-grapple on the battlefield,
While their wounded horses howl in lamentation,
Throwing up their heads at the desolate sky;

The gray ravens and hungry vultures tear,
And carry away the long bowels of the dead,
Hanging them on the twigs of lifeless trees. . . .

O soldiers who fight long—
    Their blood varnishes the desert weeds!
But the generals who lead them on—
    They have accomplished nothing!

Li Po
Translated by Cheng Yu Sun

THE MOON AT THE FORTIFIED PASS

THE bright moon lifts from the Mountain of Heaven
In an infinite haze of cloud and sea
And the wind, that has come a thousand miles,
Beats at the Jade Pass battlements . . .
China marches its men down to Po-teng Road
While Tartar troops peer across blue waters of the bay . . .
And since not one battle famous in history
Sent all its fighters back again,
The soldiers turn round, looking toward the border,
And think of home, with wistful eyes,
And of those tonight in the upper chambers
Who toss and sigh and cannot rest.

LI PO
Translated by Witter Bynner
after Kiang Kang-hu

METRUM PARHEMIACUM TRAGICUM

O SORROWFUL and ancient days,
   Where learned ye to make sepulchres?
Who taught you all the evil ways
   Wherein to wound men's souls in wars?

Woe to that sacrificial priest,
   First craftsman of the blacksmith's forge,
Who saw strange shapes within his fire,
   And hammered out illgotten swords.

[45]

Whoever fashioned first the bow,
  And flight of arrows, swift, secure,
Launched anger on the air and made
  The bitterness of death more sure.

Who tempered spearheads for their work,
  He breathed upon the anvil death;
He hammered out the slender blade,
  And from the body crushed the breath.

He gave to death a thrusting spear,
  Who first drew up his battle-hosts.
Long since hath fared his vaunting soul
  To dwell a ghost amid the ghosts.

Eugenius Vulgarius
Translated by Helen Waddell

PART TWO

THE DANCE OF THE SWORD

from THE ANCIENT BRETON

BLOOD, wine, and glee,
  Sun, to thee,—
Blood, wine, and glee!
  Fire! fire! steel, Oh! steel!
  Fire, fire! steel and fire!
  Oak! oak, earth and waves!
  Waves, oak, earth and oak!

Glee of dance and song,
  And battle-throng,—
Battle, dance, and song!
  Fire! fire! steel, etc.

Let the sword blades swing
  In a ring,—
Let the sword blades swing!
  Fire! fire! steel, etc.

Song of the blue steel,
  Death to feel,—
Song of the blue steel,
  Fire! fire! steel, etc.

Fight, whereof the sword
  Is the Lord,—
Fight of the fell sword!
  Fire! fire! steel, etc.

[48]

Sword, thou mighty king
  Of battle's ring,—
Sword thou mighty king!
  Fire! fire! steel, etc.

With the rainbow's light
  Be thou bright,—
With the rainbow's light!
  Fire! fire! steel, Oh! steel!
  Fire, fire! steel and fire!
  Oak! oak, earth and waves!
  Waves, oak, earth and oak!

ANONYMOUS
Translated by Tom Taylor

THE APPROACH OF PHARAOH

from GENESIS

. . . Then they saw
Forth and forward faring, Pharaoh's war array,
Gliding on, a grove of spears; glittering the hosts!
Fluttered there the banners, there the folk the march trod.
Onwards surged the war, strode the spears along,
Flickered the broad shields; blew aloud the trumpets.
Wheeling round in gyres, yelled the fowls of war,
Of the battle greedy; hoarsely barked the raven,
Dew upon his feathers, o'er the fallen corpses;

[49]

Swart that chooser of the slain! Sang aloud the wolves
At the eve their horrid song, hoping for the carrion
Kindless were the beasts, cruelly they threaten;
Death did these march-warders, all the midnight through,
Howl along the hostile trail—hideous slaughter of the host.

CAEDMON

THE BATTLE OF BRUNANBURH

Æthelstan King,
Lord among Earls,
Bracelet-bestower and
Baron of Barons,
He with his brother,
Edmund Atheling,
Gaining a lifelong
Glory in battle,
Slew with the sword-edge
There by Brunanburh,
Brake the shield-wall,
Hewed the linden-wood,
Hacked the battle-shield,
Sons of Edward with hammered brands.

II

Theirs was a greatness
Got from their grandsires—
Theirs that so often in
Strife with their enemies
Struck for their hoards and their hearths and their homes.

[50]

III

Bowed the spoiler,
Bent the Scotsman,
Fell the ship-crews
Doomed to the death.
All the field with blood of the fighters
Flowed, from when first the great
Sun-star of morning-tide,
Lamp of the Lord God,
Lord everlasting,
Glowed over earth till the glorious creature
Sank to his setting.

IV

There lay many a man
Marred by the javelin,
Men of the Northland
Shot over shield.
There was the Scotsman
Weary of war.

V

We the West-Saxons
Long in the daylight
Lasted, in companies
Troubled the track of the host that we hated.
Grimly with swords that were sharp from the grindstone,
Fiercely we hacked at the flyers before us.

VI

Mighty the Mercian,
Hard was his hand-play,
Sparing not any of

[51]

Those that with Anlaf
Warriors over the
Weltering waters
Borne in the bark's-bosom,
Drew to this island—
Doomed to the death.

VII

Five young kings put asleep by the sword-stroke,
Seven strong Earls of the army of Anlaf
Fell on the war-field, numberless numbers,
Shipmen and Scotsmen.

VIII

Then the Norse leader,
Dire was his need of it,
Few were his following,
Fled to his war-ship;
Fleeted his vessel to sea with the king in it,
Saving his life on the fallow flood.

IX

Also the crafty one,
Constantinus,
Crept to his North again,
Hoar-headed hero!

X

Slender warrant had
He to be proud of
The welcome of war-knives—
He that was reft of his
Folk and his friends that had

Fallen in conflict,
Leaving his son too
Lost in the carnage,
Mangled to morsels.
A youngster in war!

XI

Slender reason had
He to be glad of
The clash of the war-glaive—
Traitor and trickster
And spurner of treaties—
He nor had Anlaf
With armies so broken
A reason for bragging
That they had the better
In perils of battle
On places of slaughter—
The struggle of standards,
The rush of the javelins,
The crash of the charges,
The wielding of weapons—
The play that they played with
The children of Edward.

XII

Then with their nailed prows
Parted the Norsemen, a
Blood-reddened relic of
Javelins over
The jarring breaker, the deep-sea billow,
Shaping their way toward Dyflen again,
Shamed in their souls.

[53]

XIII

Also the brethren,
King and Atheling,
Each in his glory,
Went to his own in his own West-Saxonland,
Glad of the war.

XIV

Many a carcase they left to be carrion,
Many a livid one, many a sallow-skin—
Left for the white-tailed eagle to tear it, and
Left for the horny-nibbed raven to rend it, and
Gave to the garbagin war-hawk to gorge it, and
That gray beast, the wolf of the weald.

XV

Never had hunger
Slaughter of heroes
Slain by the sword-edge—
Such as old writers
Have writ of in histories—
Hapt in this isle, since
Up from the East hither
Saxon and Angle from
Over the broad billow
Broke into Britain with
Haughty war-workers who
Harried the Welshman, when
Earls that were lured by the
Hunger of glory gat
Hold of the land.

ANONYMOUS
Translated by Alfred, Lord Tennyson

[54]

THE SONG OF THE VALKYRIES

Widely is flung,   warning of slaughter,
the weaver's beam's-web: 'tis wet with blood;
is spread now, grey,   the spear-thing before,
the woof-of-the-warriors   which valkyries fill
with the red-warp of-   Randver's-banesman.

Is this web woven   and wound of entrails,
and heavy weighted   with heads of slain;
are blood-bespattered   spears the treadles,
iron-bound the beams,   the battens, arrows:
let us weave with our swords   this web of victory!

Goes Hild to weave,   and Hiorthrimul,
Sangrith and Svipul,   with swords brandished:
shields will be shattered,   shafts will be splintered,
will the hound-of-helmets   the hauberks bite.

Wind we, wind we   the web-of-darts,
and follow the atheling   after to war!
Will men behold   shields hewn and bloody
where Gunn and Gondul   have guarded the thane.

Wind we, wind we   such web-of-darts
as the young war-worker   waged afore-time!
Forth shall we fare   where the fray is thickest,
where friends and fellows   'gainst foemen battle!

Wind we, wind we   the web-of-darts
where float the flags   of unflinching men!
Let not the liege's   life be taken:
valkyries award   the weird of battle.

Will seafaring men   hold sway over lands,
who erstwhile dwelled   on outer nesses;
is doomed to die   a doughty king;
lies slain an earl   by swords e'en now.

Will Irish men eke   much ill abide:
'twill not ever after   be out of men's minds.
Now the web is woven,   and weapons reddened—
in all lands will be heard   the heroes' fall.

Now awful is it .   to be without,
as blood-red rack   races overhead;
is the welkin gory   with warriors' blood
as we valkyries   war-songs chanted.

Well have we chanted   charms full many
about the king's son: may it bode him well!
Let him learn them   who listens to us,
and speak these spells   to spearmen after.

Start we swiftly   with steeds unsaddled—
hence to battle   with brandished swords!

ANONYMOUS
Translated by Lee M. Hollander

INSCRIPTIONS AT THE CITY OF BRASS

from THE 1001 NIGHTS

ENTER and learn the story of the rulers,
They rested a little in the shadow of my towers

[56]

And then they passed.
They were dispersed like those shadows
When the sun goes down;
They were driven like straws
Before the wind of death.

❋

O sons of men,
You add the future to the future
But your sum is spoiled
By the gray cypher of death.
There is a Master
Who breathes upon armies,
Building a narrow and dark house for kings.
These wake above their dust
In a black commonwealth.

O sons of men,
Why do you put your hands before your eyes
And play in this road as if for ever,
Which is a short passing to another place?
Where are the kings
Whose loins jetted empires,
Where are the very strong men,
Masters of Irak?
Where are the lords of Ispahan,
O sons of men?

ANONYMOUS
Translated by E. Powys Mathers

"READY THEY MAKE HAUBERKS SARRAZINESE"

from THE SONG OF ROLAND

READY they make hauberks Sarrazinese,
That folded are, the greater part, in three;
And they lace on good helms Sarragucese;
Gird on their swords of tried steel Viennese;
Fine shields they have, and spears Valentinese,
And white, blue, red, their ensigns take the breeze,
They've left their mules behind, and their palfreys,
Their chargers mount, and canter knee by knee.
Fair shines the sun, the day is bright and clear,
Light burns again from all their polished gear.
A thousand horns they sound, more proud to seem;
Great is the noise, the Franks its echo hear.
Says Oliver: "Companion, I believe,
Sarrazins now in battle must we meet."
Answers Rollanz: "God grant us then the fee!
For our king's sake well must we quit us here;
Man for his lord should suffer great disease,
Most bitter cold endure, and burning heat,
His hair and skin should offer up at need.
Now must we each lay on most hardily,
So evil songs ne'er sung of us shall be.
Pagans are wrong: Christians are right indeed.
Evil example will never come of me."

A O I.

Marsile's nephew, his name is Aelroth,
First of them all canters before the host,
Says of our Franks these ill words as he goes:
"Felons of France, so here on us you close!
Betrayed you has he that to guard you ought;
Mad is the King who left you in this post.
So shall the fame of France the Douce be lost,
And the right arm from Charle's body torn."
When Rollant hears, what rage he has, by God!
His steed he spurs, gallops with great effort;
He goes, that count, to strike with all his force,
That shield he breaks, the hauberk's seam unsews,
Slices the heart, and shatters up the bones,
All of the spine he severs with that blow,
And with his spear the soul from body throws
So well he's pinned, he shakes in the air that corse,
On his spear's hilt he's flung it from the horse:
So in two halves Aelroth's neck he broke,
Nor left him yet, they say, but rather spoke:
"Avaunt, culvert! A madman Charles is not,
No treachery was ever in his thought.
Proudly he did, who left us in this post;
The fame of France the Douce shall not be lost.
Strike on, the Franks! Ours are the foremost blows.
For we are right, but these gluttons are wrong."

A O I.

And his comrade Gerers strikes the admiral,
The shield he breaks, the hauberk unmetals,
And his good spear drives into his vitals,
So well he's pinned him, clean through the carcass,

[59]

Dead on the field he's flung him from his hand.
Says Oliver: "Now is our battle grand."

XCVIII

Sansun the Duke goes strike that almacour,
The shield he breaks, with golden flowers tooled,
That good hauberk for him is nothing proof,
He's sliced the heart, the lungs and liver through,
And flung him dead, as well or ill may prove.
Says the Archbishop: "A baron's stroke, in truth."

XCIX

And Anseis has let his charger run;
He goes to strike Turgis of Turtelus,
The shield he breaks, its golden boss above,
The hauberk too, its doubled mail undoes,
His good spear's point into the carcass runs,
So well he's thrust, clean through the whole steel comes,
And from the hilt he's thrown him dead in dust.
Then says Rollant: "Great prowess in that thrust."

CIV

Common the fight is now and marvellous.
The count Rollanz no way himself secures,
Strikes with his spear, long as the shaft endures,
By fifteen blows it is clean broken through;
Then Durendal he bares, his sabre good
Spurs on his horse, is gone to strike Chernuble,
The helmet breaks, where bright carbuncles grew,
Slices the cap and shears the locks in two, ·
Slices also the eyes and the features,
The hauberk white, whose mail was close of woof,
Down to the groin cuts all his body through
To the saddle; with beaten gold 'twas tooled.

[60]

Upon the horse that sword a moment stood,
Then sliced its spine, no joint there any knew,
Dead in the field among thick grass them threw.
After he said. "Culbert false step you moved,
From Mahumet your help will not come soon.
No victory for gluttons such as you."

CL

Oliver feels death's anguish on him now;
And in his head his two eyes swimming round;
Nothing he sees; he hears not any sound;
Dismounting then, he kneels upon the ground,
Proclaims his sins both firmly and aloud,
Clasps his two hands, heavenwards holds them out,
Prays God himself in Paradise to allow;
Blessings on Charles, and on Douce France he vows,
And his comrade, Rollanz, to whom he's bound.
Then his heart fails; his helmet nods and bows;
Upon the earth he lays his whole length out:
And he is dead, may stay no more, that count.
Rollanz the brave mourns him with grief profound;
Nowhere on earth so sad a man you'd found.

CCXL

Clear is the day, and the sun radiant;
The hosts are fair, the companies are grand.
The first columns are come now hand to hand.
The count Rabel and the count Guinemans
Let fall the reins on their swift horses' backs,
Spurring in haste; then on rush all the Franks,
And go to strike, each with his trenchant lance.

A O I.

ANONYMOUS
Translated by H. Scott-Moncrieff

[61]

SONG OF BATTLE

Well pleaseth me the sweet time of Easter
That maketh the leaf and the flower come out.
And it pleaseth me when I hear the clamor
Of the birds' bruit about their song through the wood;
And it pleaseth me when I see through the meadows
The tents and pavilions set up, and great joy have I
When I see o'er the campana knights armed and horses
    arrayed.

And it pleaseth me when the scouts set in flight the folk with
    their goods;
And it pleaseth me when I see coming together after them an
    host of armed men.
And it pleaseth me to the heart when I see strong castles
    besieged,
And barriers broken and riven, and I see the host on the shore
    all about shut in with ditches,
And closed in with "lisses" of strong piles.

Bertrans de Born
Translated by Ezra Pound

WHEN THE TROOPS WERE RETURNING FROM MILAN

If you could see, fair brother, how dead beat
    The fellows look who come through Rome today,—
    Black yellow smoke-dried visages,—you'd say
They thought their haste at going all too fleet.

Their empty victual-wagons up the street
    Over the bridge dreadfully sound and sway;
    Their eyes, as hanged men's, turning the wrong way;
And nothing on their backs, or heads, or feet.
One sees the ribs and all the skeletons
    Of their gaunt horses; and a sorry sight
Are the torn saddles, crammed with straw and stones.
    They are ashamed, and march throughout the night;
Stumbling, for hunger, on their marrowbones;
    Like barrels rolling, jolting, in this plight.
Their arms all gone, not even their swords are saved;
And each as silent as a man being shaved.

NICCOLO DEGLI ALBIZZI
Translated by D. G. Rossetti

"MY LIEGE, I DID DENY NO PRISONERS"

from KING HENRY IV, Part I

MY LIEGE, I did deny no prisoners.
But I remember, when the fight was done,
When I was dry with rage and extreme toil,
Breathless and faint, leaning upon my sword,
Came there a certain lord, neat, and trimly dress'd,
Fresh as a bridegroom; and his chin new reap'd
Show'd like a stubble-land at harvest-home;
He was perfumed like a milliner;
And twixt his finger and his thumb he held
A pouncet-box, which ever and anon
He gave his nose and took't away again;

[63]

Who therewith angry, when it next came there,
Took it in snuff; and still he smiled and talk'd,
And as the soldiers bore dead bodies by,
He call'd them untaught knaves, unmannerly,
To bring a slovenly unhandsome corse
Betwixt the wind and his nobility.
With many holiday and lady terms
He question'd me; amongst the rest, demanded
My prisoners in your majesty's behalf.
I then, all smarting with my wounds being cold,
To be pester'd with a popinjay,
Out of my grief and my impatience,
Answer'd neglectingly I know not what,
He should or he should not; for he made me mad
To see him shine so brisk and smell so sweet
And talk so like a waiting-gentlewoman
Of guns and drums and wounds,—God save the mark!—
And telling me the sovereign'st thing on earth
Was parmaceti for an inward bruise;
And that it was great pity, so it was,
This villanous salt-petre should be digg'd
Out of the bowels of the harmless earth,
Which many a good tall fellow had destroy'd
So cowardly; and but for these vile guns,
He would himself have been a soldier.
This bald unjointed chat of his, my lord,
I answer'd indirectly, as I said;
And I beseech you, let not his report
Come current for an accusation
Betwixt my love and your high majesty.

WILLIAM SHAKESPEARE

[64]

"ONCE MORE INTO THE BREACH, DEAR FRIENDS, ONCE MORE"

from KING HENRY V

Once more into the breach, dear friends, once more;
Or close the wall up with our English dead!
In peace there's nothing so becomes a man
As modest stillness and humility:
But when the blast of war blows in our ears,
Then imitate the action of the tiger;
Stiffen the sinews, summon up the blood,
Disguise fair nature with hard-favored rage:
Then lend the eye a terrible aspect;
Let it pry through the portage of the head
Like the brass cannon; let the brow o'erwhelm it
As fearfully as doth a galled rock
O'erhang and jutty his confounded base,
Swilled with the wild and wasteful ocean.
Now set the teeth and stretch the nostril wide;
Hold hard the breath, and bend up every spirit
To his full height!—On, on, you noble English,
Whose blood is fet from fathers of war-proof!—
Fathers that, like so many Alexanders,
Have in these parts from morn to even fought,
And sheathed their swords for lack of argument.
Dishonor not your mothers; now attest
That those whom you called fathers did beget you!
Be copy now to men of grosser blood,
And teach them how to war!—And you, good yeomen,
Whose limbs were made in England, show us here
The mettle of your pasture; let us swear

[65]

That you are worth your breeding: which I doubt not;
For there is none of you so mean and base,
That hath not noble lustre in your eyes.
I see you stand like greyhounds in the slips,
Straining upon the start. The game's afoot:
Follow your spirit; and upon this charge,
Cry "God for Harry, England, and Saint George!"

WILLIAM SHAKESPEARE

"NOW ENTERTAIN CONJECTURE OF A TIME"

from KING HENRY V

Chorus: Now entertain conjecture of a time,
When creeping murmur, and the poring dark,
Fills the wide vessel of the universe.
From camp to camp, through the foul womb of night,
The hum of either army stilly sounds,
That the fixed sentinels almost receive
The secret whispers of each other's watch.
Fire answers fire; and through their paly flames
Each battle sees the other's umbered face.
Steed threatens steed in high and boastful neighs,
Piercing the night's dull ear: and from the tents,
The armorers, accomplishing the knights,
With busy hammers closing rivets up,
Give dreadful note of preparation.
The country cocks do crow, the clocks do toll,
And the third hour of drowsy morning name.
Proud of their numbers, and secure in soul,

The confident and over-lusty French
Do the low-rated English play at dice;
And chide the cripple, tardy-gaited night,
Who, like a foul and ugly witch, doth limp
So tediously away. The poor, condemned English,
Like sacrifices, by their watchful fires
Sit patiently, and inly ruminate
The morning's danger; and their gestures sad,
Investing lank-lean cheeks, and war-torn coats,
Presenteth them unto the gazing moon
So many horrid ghosts. O, now, who will behold
The royal captain of this ruined band,
Walking from watch to watch, from tent to tent,
Let him cry—Praise and glory on his head!
For forth he goes, and visits all his host;
Bids them good morrow, with a modest smile;
And calls them—brothers, friends, and countrymen.
Upon his royal face there is no note,
How dread an army hath enrounded him;
Nor doth he dedicate one jot of color
Unto the weary and all-watched night;
But freshly looks, and over-bears attaint,
With cheerful semblance and sweet majesty;
That every wretch, pining and pale before,
Beholding him, plucks comfort from his looks.
A largess universal, like the sun,
His liberal eye doth give to every one,
Thawing cold fear. Then, mean and gentle all,
Behold, as may unworthiness define,
A little touch of Harry in the night.
And so our scene must to the battle fly;
Where (O for pity!) we shall much disgrace—
With four or five most ragged foils,

Right ill-disposed, in brawl ridiculous—
The name of Agincourt. Yet, sit and see;
Minding true things, by what their mockeries be.

WILLIAM SHAKESPEARE

"GOOD SIR, WHOSE POWERS ARE THESE?"

from HAMLET, ACT IV. SC. I

HAMLET: Good sir, whose powers are these?

CAPTAIN: They are of Norway, sir.

HAM. How purposed, sir, I pray you?

CAP. Against some part of Poland.

HAM. Who commands them, sir?

CAP. The nephew to old Norway, Fortinbras.

HAM. Goes it against the main of Poland, sir,
Or for some frontier?

CAP. Truly to speak, and with no addition,
We go to gain a little patch of ground
That hath in it no profit but the name.
To pay five ducats, five, I would not farm it;
Nor will it yield to Norway or the Pole
A ranker rate, should it be sold in fee.

HAM. Why, then the Polack never will defend it.

CAP. Yes, it is already garrison'd.

HAM. Two thousand souls and twenty thousand ducats
Will not debate the question of this straw:
This is the imposthume of much wealth and peace,
That inward breaks, and shows no cause without
Why the man dies.

[68]

Examples gross as earth exhort me:
Witness this army of such mass and charge
Led by a delicate and tender prince,
Whose spirit with divine ambition puff'd
Makes mouths at the invisible event,
Exposing what is mortal and unsure
To all that fortune, death and danger dare,
Even for an egg-shell. Rightly to be great
Is not to stir without great argument,
But greatly to find quarrel in a straw
When honor's at the stake. How stand I then,
That have a father kill'd, a mother stain'd,
Excitements of my reason and my blood,
And let all sleep? while, to my shame, I see
The imminent death of twenty thousand men,
That, for a fantasy and trick of fame,
Go to their graves like beds, fight for a plot
Whereon the numbers cannot try the cause,
Which is not tomb enough and continent
To hide the slain? O, from this time forth,
My thoughts be bloody, or be nothing worth!

WILLIAM SHAKESPEARE

A BURNT SHIP

Out of a fired ship, which, by no way
But drowning, could be rescued from the flame,
Some men leap'd forth, and ever as they came
Near the foes' ships, did by their shot decay;

[69]

So all were lost, which in the ship were found,
>They in the sea being burnt, they in the burnt ship
>drowned.

JOHN DONNE

"WALKING NEXT DAY UPON THE FATAL SHORE"

from THE ATHEIST'S TRAGEDY

WALKING next day upon the fatal shore,
Among the slaughtered bodies of our men
Which the full-stomached sea had cast upon
The sands, it was my unhappy chance to light
Upon a face, whose favour when it lived,
My astonished mind informed me I had seen.
He lay in's armour, as if that had been
His coffin; and the weeping sea, like one
Whose milder temper doth lament the death
Of him whom in his rage he slew, runs up
The shore, embraces him, kisses his cheek,
Goes back again, and forces up the sands
To bury him, and every time it parts
Sheds tears upon him, till at last (as if
It could no longer endure to see the man
Whom it had slain, yet loath to leave him) with
A kind of unresolved unwilling pace,
Winding her waves one in another, like
A man that folds his arms or wrings his hands
For grief, ebbed from the body, and descends

As if it would sink down into the earth,
And hide itself for shame of such a deed.

CYRIL TOURNEUR

"THE GLORIES OF OUR BLOOD AND STATE"

from AJAX AND ULYSSES

THE glories of our blood and state
  Are shadows, not substantial things;
There is no armor against fate;
  Death lays his icy hand on kings:
      Sceptre and crown
      Must tumble down,
And in the dust be equal made
With the poor crooked scythe and spade.

Some men with swords may reap the field,
  And plant fresh laurels where they kill:
But their strong nerves at last must yield;
  They tame but one another still:
      Early or late
      They stoop to fate,
And must give up their murmuring breath
When they, pale captives, creep to death.

The garlands wither on your brow;
  Then boast no more your mighty deeds;
Upon Death's purple altar now

[71]

See where the victor-victim bleeds:
Your heads must come
To the cold tomb.
Only the actions of the just
Smell sweet, and blossom in their dust.

JAMES SHIRLEY

ON THE LATE MASSACRE IN PIEDMONT

AVENGE, O Lord, thy slaughtered saints, whose bones
Lie scattered on the Alpine mountains cold;
Even them who kept thy truth so pure of old,
When all our fathers worshipped stocks and stones,
Forget not: in thy book record their groans
Who were thy sheep, and in their ancient fold
Slain by the bloody Piedmontese that rolled
Mother with infant down the rocks. Their moans
The vales redoubled to the hills, and they
To heaven. Their martyred blood and ashes sow
O'er all the Italian fields, where still doth sway
The triple Tyrant; that from these may grow
A hundredfold, who, having learnt thy way
Early may fly the Babylonian woe.

JOHN MILTON

O STRASSBURG

GERMAN FOLK SONG

O STRASSBURG, O Strassburg,
City fine and brave!
How many and many a soldier
You've shovelled in his grave!

How many a one, so handsome
And bold as he can be,
His father and dear mother
Deserted wickedly.

Forsaken, forsaken,
It can't be otherwise.
For Strassburg, for Strassburg,
The soldier lives and dies.

The father, the mother
Go to the Captain's door:
'O Captain, dear Captain,
Give us our son once more!

'For many a golden penny
Your son I cannot yield.
Your son must go a-marching
The far broad field.

'In far field, in broad field,
Face against the foe,
Even though his nut-brown maiden
Is wailing in her woe!'

[73]

With yearning, with mourning,
Her heart is all too sore:
'Farewell, farewell, my darling,
I'll never see thee more!'
Anonymous
Translated by C. F. MacIntyre

ALL THAT IS LEFT

Old battle field, fresh with Spring flowers again—
All that is left of the dream
Of twice ten thousand warriors slain.
Bashō
Translated by Curtis Hidden Page

THE MAUNDING SOLDIER

Or, THE FRUITS OF WARRE IS BEGGERY

Good, your worship, cast your eyes
Upon a souldier's miseries!
Let not my leane cheekes, I pray,
Your bounty from a souldier stay,
    But, like a noble friend,
    Some silver lend,
And Jove shall pay you in the end:
    And I will pray that Fate
    May make you fortunate
In heavenly, and in earth's estate.

[74]

To beg I was not borne, sweet Sir,
And therefore blush to make this stirre;
I never went from place to place
For to divulge my wofull case:
      For I am none of those
      That roguing goes,
That, maunding, shewes their drunken blowes,
      Which they have onely got
      While they have bang'd the pot
In wrangling who should pay the shot.

I scorne to make comparison
With those of Kent-street garrison,
That in their lives nere crost the seas,
But still at home have lived at ease;
      Yet will they lye and sweare,
      As though they were
Men that travel'd farre and neere;
      True souldiers' company
      Doth teach them how to lye;
They can discourse most perfectly.

But I doe scorne such counterfaits
That get their meanes by base deceits:
They learne of other to speake Dutch;
Of Holland they'll tell you as much
      As those that have bin there
      Fule many a yeere,
And name the townes all farre and neere;
      Yet they never' went
      Beyond Graves-end in Kent,
But in Kent-*street* their dayes are spent.

[75]

(They) in Olympicke games have beene,
Whereas brave battels I have seene;
And where the cannon(s) used to roare
My proper spheare was evermore;
    The danger I have past,
    Both first and last,
Would make your worship's selfe agast;
    A thousand times I have
    Been ready for the grave;
Three times I have been made a slave.

Twice through the bulke I have been shot;
My brains have boyl'd like a pot:
I have at lest these doozen times
Been blowne up by those roguish mines
    Under a barracado,
    In a bravado,
Throwing of a hand-granado;
    Oh! death was very neere,
    For it took away my eare,
And yet, thanke God! ch'am here, ch'am here.

I have upon the seas been tane
By th' Dunkerks, for the King of Spaine,
And stript out of my garments quite,
Exchanging all for canvis white;
    And in that pore aray
    For many a day
I have been kept, till friends did pay
    A ransome for release;
    And having bought my peace,
My woes againe did fresh increase.

[76]

There's no land-service as you can name
But I have been actor in the same;
In th' Palatinate and Bohemia
I served many a wofull day;
      At Frankendale I have,
      Like a souldier brave
Receiv'd what welcomes canons gave;
      For the honour of England
      Most stoutly did I stand
Gainst the Emperour's and Spinolae's band.

At push of pike I lost mine eye;
At Bergen siege I broke my thigh;
At Ostend, though I were a lad,
I laid about me as I were mad.
      Oh, you would little ween
      That I had been
An old, old souldier to the Queene;
      But if Sir Francis Vere
      Were living now and here,
Hee'd tell you how I slasht it there.

Since that, I have been in Breda
Besieg'd by Marquese Spinola;
And, since that, made a warlike dance
Both into Spaine and into France;
      And there I lost a flood
      Of noble blood,
And did but very little good:
      And now I home am come,
      With ragges about my bumme,
God bless you, Sir, from this poore summe!

And now my case you understand,
Good Sir, will you lend your helping hand?
A little thing will pleasure me,
And keepe in use your charity:
      It is not bread nor cheese,
      Nor barrell lees,
Nor any scraps of meat, like these;
      But I doe beg of you
      A shilling or two,
Sweet Sir, your purse's strings undoe.

I pray your worship, thinke on me,
That am what I doe seeme to be—
No rooking rascall, nor no cheat,
But a souldier every way compleat;
      I have wounds to show
      That prove 'tis so;
Then courteous good Sir, ease my woe;
      And I for you will pray
      Both night and day
That your substance never may decay.

MARTIN PARKER

PLAYTHINGS

GREAT princes have great playthings. Some
      have played
At hewing mountains into men, and some
At building human wonders mountain high.
Some have amassed the dull sad years of life

(Life spent in indolence, and therefore sad)
With schemes of monumental fame, and sought
By pyramids and mausolean pomp,
Short-lived themselves, t'immortalize their bones.
Some seek diversion in the tented field
And make the sorrows of mankind their sport.
But war's a game which, were their subjects wise,
Kings should not play at. Nations would do well
T'exhort their truncheons from the puny hands
Of heroes, whose infirm and baby minds
Are gratified with mischief, and who spoil,
Because men suffer it, their toy the world.

WILLIAM COWPER

A WAR SONG TO ENGLISHMEN

PREPARE, prepare the iron helm of War,
Bring forth the lots, cast in the spacious orb;
The Angel of Fate turns them with mighty hands,
And casts them out upon the darkened earth!
                    Prepare, prepare!

Prepare your hearts for Death's cold hand! prepare
Your souls for flight, your bodies for the earth;
Prepare your arms for glorious victory;
Prepare your eyes to meet a holy God!
                    Prepare, prepare!

Whose fatal scroll is that? Methinks 'tis mine!
Why sinks my heart, why faltereth my tongue?

[79]

Had I three lives, I'd die in such a cause,
And rise, with ghosts, over the well-fought field.
                              Prepare, prepare!

The arrows of Almighty God are drawn!
Angels of Death stand in the lowering heavens!
Thousands of souls must seek the realms of light,
And walk together on the clouds of heaven!
                              Prepare, prepare!

Soldiers, prepare! Our cause is Heaven's cause;
Soldiers, prepare! Be worthy of our cause:
Prepare to meet our fathers in the sky:
Prepare, O troops, that are to fall to-day!
                              Prepare, prepare!

Alfred shall smile, and make his harp rejoice;
The Norman William, and the learned Clerk,
And Lion Heart, and black-browed Edward, with
His loyal Queen, shall rise, and welcome us!
                              Prepare, prepare!
                                   WILLIAM BLAKE

JERUSALEM

from MILTON

AND did those feet in ancient time
    Walk upon England's mountains green?
And was the holy Lamb of God
    On England's pleasant pastures seen?

[80]

And did the Countenance Divine
   Shine forth upon our clouded hills?
And was Jerusalem builded here
   Among these dark Satanic Mills?

Bring me my bow of burning gold!
   Bring me my arrows of desire!
Bring me my spear! O clouds, unfold!
   Bring me my chariot of fire!

I will not cease from mental fight,
   Nor shall my sword sleep in my hand,
Till we have built Jerusalem
   In England's green and pleasant land.

                    WILLIAM BLAKE

THE FRENCH AND THE SPANISH GUERRILLAS

HUNGER, and sultry heat, and nipping blast
From bleak hill-top, and length of march by night
Through heavy swamp, or over snow-clad height—
These hardships ill-sustained, these dangers past,
The roving Spanish Bands are reached at last,
Charged, and dispersed like foam: but as a flight
Of scattered quails by signs do reunite,
So these,—and, heard of once again, are chased
With combinations of long-practised art
And newly-kindled hope; but they are fled—
Gone are they, viewless as the buried dead:

[81]

Where now?—Their sword is at the Foeman's heart!
And thus from year to year his walk they thwart,
And hang like dreams around his guilty bed.

WILLIAM WORDSWORTH

THE AMERICAN HERO

A SAPPHIC ODE

WHY should vain Mortals tremble at the sight of
Death and Destruction in the Field of Battle,
Where Blood and Carnage clothe the Ground in Crimson,
    Sounding with Death Groans?

Death will invade us by the Means appointed,
And we must all bow to the King of Terrors;
Nor am I anxious, if I am prepared,
    What Shape he comes in.

Infinite Goodness teaches us Submission;
Bids us be quiet under all his Dealings:
Never repining, but forever praising
    God our Creator.

Well may we praise him, all his Ways are perfect:
Though a Resplendence infinitely glowing,
Dazzles in Glory on the Sight of Mortals
    Struck blind by Lustre!

Good is Jehovah in bestowing Sunshine,
Nor less his Goodness in the Storm and Thunder:

Mercies and Judgments both proceed from Kindness . . .
                    Infinite Kindness!

O then exult, that God forever reigneth
Clouds, which around him hinder our Perception,
Bind us the stronger to exalt his Name, and
                    Shout louder Praises!

Then to the wisdom of my Lord and Master,
I will commit all that I have or wish for:
Sweetly as babes sleep will I give my life up
                    When call'd to yield it.

Now, *Mars*, I dare thee, clad in smoky pillars,
Bursting from bomb-shells, roaring from the cannon,
Rattling in grape shot, like a storm of hailstones,
                    Torturing aether!

Up the bleak heavens let the spreading flames rise
Breaking like Aetna through the smoky columns,
Low'ring like Egypt o'er the falling city
                    Wantonly burnt down.

While all their hearts quick palpitate for havock,
Let slip your blood hounds, nam'd the British lyons;
Dauntless as death stares; nimble as the whirlwind;
                    Dreadful as demons!

Let oceans waft on all your floating castles;
Fraught with destruction, horrible to nature:
Then, with your sails fill'd by a storm of vengeance,
                    Bear down to battle!

[83]

From the dire caverns made by ghostly miners,
Let the explosion, dreadful as vulcanoes,
Heave the broad town, with all its wealth and people,
                    Quick to destruction!

Still shall the banner of the King of Heaven
Never advance where I'm afraid to follow:
While that precedes me with an open bosom,
                    War, I defy thee.

Fame and dear freedom *lure* me on to battle.
While a fell despot, grimer than a death's-head,
Stings me with serpents, fiercer than Medusa's:
                    To the encounter.

Life, for my country and the cause of freedom,
Is but a trifle for a worm to part with;
And if preservéd in so great a contest,
                    Life is redoubled.

                              NATHANIEL NILES

HOHENLINDEN

On LINDEN when the sun was low,
All bloodless lay the untrodden snow,
And dark as winter was the flow
Of Iser rolling rapidly!
But Linden show'd another sight
When the drum beat at dead of night,
Commanding fires of death to light
The darkness of her scenery.

[84]

By torch and trumpet fast array'd,
Each horseman drew his battle-blade,
And furious every charger neigh'd
To join the dreadful revelry!
Then shook the hills with thunder riven,
Then rush'd the steed to battle driven,
And louder than the bolts of heaven
Far flash'd the red artillery!

But redder yet that light shall glow
On Linden's hills of stainéd snow,
And bloodier yet the torrent flow
Of Iser rolling rapidly!
'Tis morn, but scarce yon level sun
Can pierce the war-clouds rolling dun,
When furious Frank and fiery Hun,
Shout in their sulphurous canopy!

The combat deepens: on, ye brave,
Who rush to glory or the grave!
Wave, Munich! all thy banners wave,
And charge with all thy chivalry.
Few, few shall part where many meet!
The snow shall be their winding-sheet,
And every turf beneath their feet
Shall be a soldier's sepulchre.

THOMAS CAMPBELL

[85]

HIGH GERMANY

'OH POLLY love, Oh Polly, the rout has now begun,
And we must march along by the beating of the drum;
Go dress yourself all in your best, and come along with me,
I'll take you to the war that's in High Germany.'

'O Harry, O Harry, you mind what I do say,
My feet they are so tender I cannot march away;
And, besides, my dearest Harry, I am in love with thee,
I'm not fitted for the cruel wars in High Germany.'

'I'll buy a horse, my love, and on it you shall ride,
And all my delight shall be riding by your side;
We'll call at every ale-house, and drink when we are dry,
So quickly on the road, my boys, we'll marry by and by.'

'O curséd were the cruel wars that ever they should rise!
And out of merry England pressed many a lad likewise;
They pressed young Harry from me, likewise my brothers
       three,
And sent them to the cruel wars in High Germany.'

ANONYMOUS

THE WAR-SONG OF DINAS VAWR

from THE MISFORTUNES OF ELPHIN

THE mountain sheep are sweeter,
But the valley sheep are fatter,

[86]

We therefore deemed it meeter
To carry off the latter.
We made an expedition;
We met a host, and quelled it;
We forced a strong position,
And killed the men who held it.

On Dyfed's richest valley,
Where herds of kine were brousing,
We made a mighty sally,
To furnish our carousing.
Fierce warriors rushed to meet us;
We met them, and o'erthrew them:
They struggled hard to beat us;
But we conquered them, and slew them.

As we drove our prize at leisure,
The king marched forth to catch us;
His rage surpassed all measure,
But his people could not match us.
He fled to his hall-pillars;
And, ere our force we led off,
Some sacked his house and cellars,
While others cut his head off.

We there, in strife bewild'ring,
Spilt blood enough to swim in:
We orphaned many children,
And widowed many women.
The eagles and the ravens
We glutted with our foemen;
The heroes and the cravens,
The spearmen and the bowmen.

[87]

We brought away from battle,
And much their land bemoaned them,
Two thousand head of cattle,
And the head of him who owned them:
Ednyfed, King of Dyfed,
His head was borne before us;
His wine and beasts supplied our feasts,
And his overthrow, our chorus.

THOMAS LOVE PEACOCK

WATERLOO

from CHILDE HAROLD'S PILGRIMAGE

THERE was a sound of revelry by night,
And Belgium's capital had gathered then
Her Beauty and her Chivalry, and bright
The lamps shone o'er fair women and brave men;
A thousand hearts beat happily; and when
Music arose with its voluptuous swell,
Soft eyes looked love to eyes which spake again,
And all went merry as a marriage bell;
But hush! hark! a deep sound strikes like a rising knell!

Did ye not hear it?—No; 'twas but the wind,
Or the car rattling o'er the stony street;
On with the dance! let joy be unconfined;
No sleep till morn, when Youth and Pleasure meet
To chase the glowing Hours with flying feet—

[88]

But hark!—that heavy sound breaks in once more,
　As if the clouds its echo would repeat;
　And nearer, clearer, deadlier than before!
Arm! Arm! it is—it is—the cannon's opening roar!

　Within a windowed niche of that high hall
　Sat Brunswick's fated chieftain; he did hear
　That sound the first amidst the festival,
　And caught its tone with Death's prophetic ear;
　And when they smiled because he deemed it near,
　His heart more truly knew that peal too well
　Which stretched his father on a bloody bier,
　And roused the vengeance blood alone could quell:
He rushed into the field, and, foremost fighting, fell.

　Ah! then and there was hurrying to and fro,
　And gathering tears, and tremblings of distress,
　And cheeks all pale, which but an hour ago
　Blushed at the praise of their own loveliness;
　And there were sudden partings, such as press
　The life from out young hearts, and choking sighs
　Which ne'er might be repeated; who could guess
　If ever more should meet those mutual eyes,
Since upon night so sweet such awful morn could rise!

　And there was mounting in hot haste—the steed,
　The mustering squadron, and the clattering car,
　Went pouring forward with impetuous speed,
　And swiftly forming in the ranks of war—
　And the deep thunder peal on peal afar;
　And near, the beat of the alarming drum
　Roused up the soldier ere the morning star;
　While thronged the citizens with terror dumb,

[89]

Or whispering, with white lips—"The foe! They come! they
  come!"

  And wild and high the *Cameron's Gathering* rose!
  The war-note of Lochiel, which Albyn's hills
  Have heard, and heard, too, have her Saxon foes:—
  How in the noon of night that pibroch thrills,
  Savage and shrill! but with the breath which fills
  Their mountain-pipe, so fill the mountaineers
  With the fierce native daring which instills
  The stirring memory of a thousand years,
And Evan's—Donald's—fame rings in each clansman's ears!

  And Ardennes waves above them her green leaves,
  Dewy with Nature's tear-drops as they pass,
  Grieving, if aught inanimate e'er grieves,
  Over the unreturning brave,—alas!
  Ere evening to be trodden like the grass
  Which now beneath them, but above shall grow
  In its next verdure, when this fiery mass
  Of living valor, rolling on the foe
And burning with high hope shall molder cold and low.

  Last noon beheld them full of lusty life,
  Last eve in Beauty's circle proudly gay,
  The midnight brought the signal-sound of strife,
  The morn the marshaling in arms,—the day
  Battle's magnificently stern array!
  The thunder-clouds close o'er it, which when rent
  The earth is covered thick with other clay,
  Which her own clay shall cover, heaped and pent,
Rider and horse,—friend, foe,—in one red burial blent!

GEORGE GORDON, LORD BYRON

[90]

THE BURIAL OF SIR JOHN MOORE
AFTER CORUNNA

Not a drum was heard, not a funeral note,
As his corse to the rampart we hurried;
Not a soldier discharged his farewell shot
O'er the grave where our hero we buried

We buried him darkly at dead of night,
The sods with our bayonets burning,
By the struggling moonbeam's misty light
And the lanthorn dimly burning.

No useless coffin enclosed his breast,
Not in sheet or in shroud we wound him;
But he lay like a warrior taking his rest
With his martial cloak around him.

Few and short were the prayers we said,
And we spoke not a word of sorrow;
But we steadfastly gazed on the face of the dead,
And we bitterly thought of the morrow.

We thought, as we hollow'd his narrow bed
And smooth'd down his lonely pillow,
That the foe and the stranger would tread o'er his head,
And we far away on the billow!

Lightly they'll talk of the spirit that's gone,
And o'er his cold ashes upbraid him—
But little he'll reck, if they let him sleep on
In the grave where a Briton has laid him.

But half of our heavy task was done
When the clock struck the hour for retiring;
And we heard the distant and random gun
That the foe was sullenly firing.

Slowly and sadly we laid him down,
From the field of his fame fresh and gory;
We carved not a line, and we raised not a stone,
But we left him alone with his glory.

CHARLES WOLFE

AFTER SIX THOUSAND YEARS

GOING on six thousand years
Angry men have had their wars;
God, a prodigal, it appears,
Made the flowers and the stars.

Contemplation of the sky,
The lily and the gilded nest,
Lent no touch of sanity
To the madness in man's breast.

Victories and bloody sack—
Of such is his love the sum;
And the multitudes in black
Move to nothing but the drum.

Under the imperial tread
Of the nightmare-freighted lorry

Lie the mothers of the dead
And their children. Such is glory.

Virtue, by its fierceness measured,
Cries: 'The time to live has passed!'
While the mouth stores up its treasured
Spittle for the trumpet-blast.

Steel gleams, bivouac fires smoulder;
—What shall pallid souls unbleach?
Shadowy spirits stand out bolder
At a cannon's fiery breach.

All for this: the ruling classes
Have you scarcely under ground,
Quietly rotting, when their glasses
Toast you to another round;

Or, when on the field of hate
Vulture wheels and jackal moans,
Gingerly investigate
To see what flesh still clothes your bones.

Tolerate no people can
That another live beside them:
Incident will be found to fan
Anger to a storm to hide them.

He's a Russian! Cut his throat.
Rolling fire is good enough
For this fellow—he's a Croat!
That one? Uniformed in buff . . .

Put the beggar out of pain,
Satisfied that all is fine
Since his crime was to remain
On the left side of the Rhine.

Rosbach! Waterloo! Cry vèngeance!
Mankind in a drunken fright
Shows no more intelligence
Than the massacre in the night.

A choice: to grow beside the fountain,
Pray in the shade upon one's knees,
Love, dream upon the mountain—
Killing one's brother is sweeter than these.

Cut, sever, butcher, stab,
Run in an ecstasy of force;
Terror's compulsion is to grab
Fistwise by its mane the horse.

Night falls, but it yields to day!
These, in truth, are wondrous things:
Hatred still maintains its sway
And the lark sings.

VICTOR HUGO
Translated by S. R.

CONCORD HYMN

Sung at the Completion of the Battle Monument,
April 19, 1836

By THE rude bridge that arched the flood,
 Their flag to April's breeze unfurled,
Here once the embattled farmers stood,
 And fired the shot heard round the world.

The foe long since in silence slept;
 Alike the conqueror silent sleeps;
And Time the ruined bridge has swept
 Down the dark stream which seaward creeps.

On this green bank, by this soft stream,
 We set today a votive stone;
That memory may their deed redeem,
 When, like our sires, our sons are gone.

Spirit, that made those heroes dare
 To die, and leave their children free,
Bid time and Nature gently spare
 The shaft we raise to them and thee.

RALPH WALDO EMERSON

THE ARSENAL AT SPRINGFIELD

THIS is the Arsenal. From floor to ceiling,
 Like a huge organ, rise the burnished arms;

[95]

But from their silent pipes no anthem pealing
　　Startles the villages with strange alarms.

Ah! what a sound will rise, how wild and dreary,
　　When the death-angel touches those swift keys!
What loud lament and dismal *Miserere*
　　Will mingle with their awful symphonies!

I hear even now the infinite fierce chorus,
　　The cries of agony, the endless groan,
Which, through the ages that have gone before us,
　　In long reverberations reach our own.

On helm and harness rings the Saxon hammer,
　　Through Cimbric forest roars the Norseman's song,
And loud, amid the universal clamor,
　　O'er distant deserts sounds the Tartar gong.

I hear the Florentine, who from his palace
　　Wheels out his battle-bell with dreadful din,
And Aztec priests upon their teocallis
　　Beat the wild war-drum made of serpent's skin;

The tumult of each sacked and burning village:
　　The shout that every prayer for mercy drowns;
The soldiers' revels in the midst of pillage;
　　The wail of famine in beleaguered towns;

The bursting shell, the gateway wrenched asunder,
　　The rattling musketry, the clashing blade;
And ever and anon, in tones of thunder,
　　The diapason of the cannonade.

Is it, O man, with such discordant noises,
  With such accursed instruments as these,
Thou drownest Nature's sweet and kindly voices,
  And jarrest the celestial harmonies?

Were half the power, that fills the world with terror,
  Were half the wealth, bestowed on camps and courts,
Given to redeem the human mind from error,
  There were no need of arsenals nor forts:

The warrior's name would be a name abhorred!
  And every nation, that should lift again
Its hand against a brother, on its forehead
  Would wear forevermore the curse of Cain!

Down the dark future, through long generations,
  The echoing sounds grow fainter and then cease;
And like a bell, with solemn, sweet vibrations,
  I hear once more the voice of Christ say, "Peace!"

Peace! and no longer from its brazen portals
  The blast of War's great organ shakes the skies!
But beautiful as songs of the immortals,
  The holy melodies of love arise.

HENRY WADSWORTH LONGFELLOW

SAY NOT THE STRUGGLE NAUGHT AVAILETH

SAY not the struggle naught availeth,
  The labour and the wounds are vain,

The enemy faints not, nor faileth,
  And as things have been they remain.

If hopes were dupes, fears may be liars;
  It may be, in yon smoke conceal'd,
Your comrades chase e'en now the fliers,
  And but for you, possess the field.

For while the tired waves, vainly breaking,
  Seem here no painful inch to gain,
Far back, through creeks and inlets making,
  Comes silent, flooding in, the main.

And not by eastern windows only,
  When daylight comes, comes in the light;
In front the sun climbs slow, how slowly!
  But westward, look, the land is bright!

ARTHUR HUGH CLOUGH

THE TEMERAIRE

(Supposed to have been suggested to an Englishman of
the old order by the fight of the "Monitor" and "Mer-
rimac.")

THE gloomy hulls, in armour grim,
  Like clouds o'er moors have met,
And prove that oak, and iron, and man
  Are tough in fibre yet.

[98]

But Splendours wane. The sea-fight yields
  No front of old display;
The garniture, emblazonment,
  And heraldry all decay.

Towering afar in parting light,
  The fleets like Albion's forelands shine—
The full-sailed fleets, the shrouded show
  Of Ships-of-the-Line.
The fighting *Temeraire*,
  Built of a thousand trees,
Lunging out her lightnings,
  And beetling o'er the seas—
O Ship, how brave and fair,
  That fought so oft and well,
On open decks you manned the gun
      Armorial.

What cheerings did you share,
  Impulsive in the van,
When down upon leagued France and Spain
  We English ran—
The freshet at your bowsprit
  Like the foam upon the can.
Bickering, your colours
  Licked up the Spanish air,
You flapped with flames of battle-flags—
  Your challenge, *Temeraire!*
The rear ones of our fleet
  They yearned to share your place,
Still vying with the *Victory*
  Throughout that earnest race—

The *Victory,* whose Admiral,
    With orders nobly won,
Shone in the globe of the battle glow—
    The angel in that sun.
Parallel in story,
    Lo, the stately pair,
As late in grapple ranging,
    The foe between them there—
When four great hulls lay tiered,
And the fiery tempest cleared,
And your prizes twain appeared,
        Temeraire!

But Trafalgar is over now,
    The quarter-deck undone;
The carved and castled navies fire
    Their evening-gun.
O, Titan *Temeraire,*
    Your stern-lights fade away;
Your bulwarks to the years must yield,
    And heart-of-oak decay.
A pigmy steam-tug tows you,
    Gigantic to the shore—
Dismantled of your guns and spars,
    And sweeping wings of war.

The rivets clinch the ironclads,
    Men learn a deadlier lore;
But Fame has nailed your battle-flags—
    Your ghost it sails before:
O, the navies old and oaken,
    O, the *Temeraire* no more!

HERMAN MELVILLE

THE MARCH INTO VIRGINIA

Ending in the First Manassas (July 1861)

Did all the lets and bars appear
   To every just or larger end,
Whence should come the trust and cheer?
   Youth must its ignorant impulse end—
Age finds place in the rear.
   All wars are boyish and are fought by boys,
The champions and enthusiasts of the state;
   Turbid ardours and vain joys
     Not barrenly abate—
   Stimulants to the power mature,
     Preparatives of fate.

Who here forecasteth the event?
What heart but spurns at precedent
And warnings of the wise,
Contemned foreclosures of surprise?
The banners play, the bugles call,
The air is blue and prodigal.
   No berrying-party, pleasure-wooed,
No picnic party in the May,
Ever went less loth than they
   Into that leafy neighborhood.
In Bacchic glee they file toward Fate,
Moloch's uninitiate;
Expectancy, and glad surmise
Of battle's unknown mysteries.
All they feel is this: 'tis glory,
A rapture sharp, though transitory,

[101]

Yet lasting in belaurelled story.
So they gaily go to fight,
Chatting left and laughing right.

But some who this blithe mood present,
    As on in lightsome files they fare,
Shall die experienced ere three days are spent—
    Perish, enlightened by the volleyed glare;
Or shame survive, and, like to adamant,
    The throes of Second Manassas share.

HERMAN MELVILLE

I HEAR AND SEE NOT STRIPS
OF CLOTH ALONE

I HEAR and see not strips of cloth alone;
I hear the tramp of armies, I hear the challenging sentry;
I hear the jubilant shouts of millions of men—I hear LIBERTY!
I hear the drums beat, and the trumpets blowing;
I myself move abroad, swift-rising, flying then;
I use the wings of the land-bird, and use the wings of the sea-
        bird, and look down as from a height;
I do not deny the precious results of peace—I see populous
        cities, with wealth incalculable;
I see numberless farms—I see the farmers working in their
        fields or barns;
I see mechanics working—I see buildings everywhere founded,
        going up, or finished;
I see trains of cars swiftly speeding along railroad tracks,
        drawn by locomotives;

[102]

I see the stores, depots, of Boston, Baltimore, Charlestown, New Orleans;
I see far in the west the immense area of grain—I dwell awhile, hovering;
I pass to the lumber forests of the north, and again to the southern plantation, and again to California;
Sweeping the whole, I see the countless profit, the busy gatherings, earned wages;
See the identity formed out of thirty-six spacious and haughty States, (and many more to come;)
See forts on the shores of harbors—see ships sailing in and out;
Then over all, (ay! ay!) my little and lengthen'd pennant shaped like a sword,
Runs swiftly up, indicating war and defiance— And now the halyards have rais'd it,
Side of my banner broad and blue—side of my starry banner,
Discarding peace over all the sea and land.

WALT WHITMAN

VIGIL STRANGE I KEPT ON THE FIELD ONE NIGHT

VIGIL strange I kept on the field one night;
When you my son and my comrade dropt at my side that day,
One look I but gave which your dear eyes return'd with a look I shall never forget,
One touch of your hand to mine O boy, reach'd up as you lay on the ground,
Then onward I sped in the battle, the even-contested battle,

[103]

Till late in the night reliev'd to the place at last again I made
my way,

Found you in death so cold dear comrade, found your body
son of responding kisses, (never again on earth respond-
ing,)

Bared your face in the starlight, curious the scene, cool blew
the moderate night-wind,

Long there and then in vigil I stood, dimly around me the
battlefield spreading,

Vigil wondrous and vigil sweet there in the fragrant silent
night,

But not a tear fell, not even a long-drawn sigh, long, long I
gazed,

Then on the earth partially reclining sat by your side leaning
my chin in my hands,

Till at latest lingering of the night, indeed just as the dawn
appear'd,

My comrade I wrapt in his blanket, envelop'd well his form,

Folded the blanket well, tucking it carefully over head and
carefully under feet,

And there and then and bathed by the rising sun, my son in
his grave, in his rude-dug grave I deposited,

Ending my vigil strange with that, vigil of night and battle-
field dim,

Vigil for boy of responding kisses, (never again on earth re-
sponding),

Vigil for comrade swiftly slain, vigil I never forget, how as day
brightened,

I rose from the chill ground and folded my soldier well in his
blanket,

And buried him where he fell.

WALT WHITMAN

I SAW THE VISION OF ARMIES

I saw the vision of armies;
And I saw, as in noiseless dreams, hundreds of battle-flags;
Borne through the smoke of the battles, and pierc'd with mis-
    siles, I saw them,
And carried hither and yon through the smoke, and torn and
    bloody;
And at last but a few shreds of the flags left on the staffs, (and
    all in silence,)
And the staffs all splinter'd and broken.

I saw battle-corpses, myriads of them,
And the white skeletons of young men—I saw them;
I saw the debris and debris of all dead soldiers;
But I saw they were not as was thought;
They themselves were fully at rest—they suffer'd not;
The living remain'd and suffer'd—the mother suffer'd,
And the wife and the child, and the musing comrade suffer'd,
And the armies that remained suffer'd.

WALT WHITMAN

RECONCILIATION

Word over all, beautiful as the sky,
Beautiful that war and all its deeds of carnage must in time be
    utterly lost,
That the hands of the sisters Death and Night incessantly
    softly wash again, and ever again, this soil'd world;

[105]

For my enemy is dead, a man divine as myself is dead,
I look where he lies white-faced and still in the coffin—I draw
near,
Bend down and touch lightly with my lips the white face in
the coffin.

WALT WHITMAN

DIRGE FOR A SOLDIER

CLOSE his eyes; his work is done!
What to him is friend or foeman,
Rise of moon, or set of sun,
Hand of man, or kiss of woman?
Lay him low, lay him low,
In the clover or the snow!
What cares he? He cannot know;
Lay him low!

As man may, he fought his fight,
Proved his truth by his endeavor;
Let him sleep in solemn night,
Sleep forever and forever.
Lay him low, lay him low,
In the clover or the snow!
What cares he? He cannot know;
Lay him low!

Fold him in his country's stars,
Roll the drum and fire the volley!
What to him are all our wars,
What but death bemocking folly?

Lay him low, lay him low,
In the clover or the snow!
What cares he? He cannot know;
   Lay him low!

Leave him to God's watching eye;
   Trust him to the hand that made him.
Mortal love weeps idly by;
   God alone has power to aid him.
   Lay him low, lay him low,
   In the clover or the snow!
   What cares he? He cannot know!
      Lay him low!

                              GEORGE HENRY BOKER

"MY TRIUMPH LASTED
TILL THE DRUMS"

My TRIUMPH lasted till the drums
Had left the Dead alone,
And then I dropped my victory
And, chastened, stole along

To where the finished faces
Conclusion turned on me—
And then I hated glory
And wished myself were They!

What is to be—is best descried
When it has also been,—

[107]

Could Prospect taste of Retrospect
The tyrannies of men

Were tenderer, diviner
The Transitive toward.
A bayonet's contrition
Is nothing to the Dead!

EMILY DICKINSON

"SUCCESS IS COUNTED SWEETEST"

Success is counted sweetest
By those who ne'er succeed.
To comprehend a nectar
Requires sorest need.

Not one of all the purple host
Who took the flag today
Can tell the definition,
So clear, of victory,

As he defeated, dying,
On whose forbidden ear
The distant strains of triumph
Break, agonized and clear.

EMILY DICKINSON

CHANNEL FIRING

That night your great guns, unawares,
Shook all our coffins as we lay,
And broke the chancel window-squares,
We thought it was the judgment-day

And sat upright. While drearisome
Arose the howl of wakened hounds:
The mouse let fall the altar-crumb,
The worms drew back into the mounds,

The glebe cow drooled. Till God called, "No;
It's gunnery practise out at sea
Just as before you went below;
The world is as it used to be:

"All nations striving strong to make
Red war yet redder. Mad as hatters
They do no more for Christés sake
Than you who are helpless in such matters.

"That this is not the judgment-hour
For some of them's a blessed thing,
For if it were they'd have to scour
Hell's floor for so much threatening . . .

"Ha, ha. It will be warmer when
I blow the trumpet (if indeed
I ever do; for you are men,
And rest eternal sorely need)."

So down we lay again. "I wonder,
Will the world ever saner be,"
Said one, "than when He sent us under
In our indifferent century!"

And many a skeleton shook his head.
"Instead of preaching forty year,"
My neighbor Parson Thirdly said,
"I wish I had stuck to pipes and beer."

Again the guns disturbed the hour,
Roaring their readiness to avenge,
As far inland as Stourton Tower,
And Camelot, and starlit Stonehenge.
April 1914

THOMAS HARDY

THE MAN HE KILLED

"Had he and I but met
  By some old ancient inn,
We should have sat us down to wet
  Right many a nipperkin!

"But ranged as infantry,
  And staring face to face,
I shot at him as he at me,
  And killed him in his place.

"I shot him dead because—
  Because he was my foe

Just so: my foe of course he was;
　　That's clear enough; although

"He thought he'd 'list, perhaps,
　　Off-hand like—just as I—
Was out of work—had sold his traps—
　　No other reason why.

"Yes; quaint and curious war is!
　　You shoot a fellow down
You'd treat if met where any bar is,
　　Or help to half-a-crown."
1902

THOMAS HARDY

FOUR LYRICS FROM THE DYNASTS

THE BOATMAN'S SONG

(The Night of Trafalgar)

In the cold October night-time, when the wind raved round
　　the land,
And the Back-sea met the Front-sea, and our doors were
　　blocked with sand,
And we heard the drub of Dead-man's Bay, where bones of
　　thousands are,
We knew not what the day had done for us at Trafalgár.
　　　　　(All) Had done,
　　　　　　　Had done,
　　　　　For us at Trafalgár!

[111]

"Pull hard, and make the Nothe, or down we go!" one says,
    says he.
We pulled; and bedtime brought the storm; but snug at home
    slept we.
Yet all the while our gallants after fighting through the day,
Were beating up and down the dark, sou'-west of Cadiz Bay.
           The dark,
           The dark,
        Sou'-west of Cadiz Bay!

The victims and the vanquished then the storm it tossed and
    tore,
As hard they strove, those worn-out men, upon that surly
    shore;
Dead Nelson and his half-dead crew, his foes from near and
    far,
Were rolled together on the deep that night at Trafalgár!
           The deep,
           The deep,
      That night at Trafalgár!

AFTER JENA

The prelude to this smooth scene—mark well!—were the
    shocks whereof the times gave token
Vaguely to us ere last year's snows shut over Lithuanian pine
    and pool,
Which we told at the fall of the faded leaf, when the pride of
    Prussia was bruised and broken
And the Man of Adventure sat in the seat of the Man of
    Method and rigid Rule.

Snows incarnadined were thine, O Eylau, field of the wide
     white spaces,
And frozen lakes, and frozen limbs, and blood iced hard as it
     left the veins:
Steel-cased squadrons swathed in cloud-drift, plunging to
     doom through pathless places,
And forty thousand dead and near-dead, strewing the early-
     nighted plains.

Friedland to these adds its tale of victims, its midnight marches
     and hot collisions,
Its plunge, at his word, on the enemy hooped by the bended
     river and famed Mill stream,
As he shatters the moves of the loose-knit nations to curb his
     exploitful soul's ambitions,
And their great Confederacy dissolves like the diorama of a
     dream.

ALBUERA

THEY come, beset by riddling hail;
They sway like sedges in a gale;
They fail, and win, and win, and fail. Albuera!

They gain the ground there, yard by yard,
Their brows and hair and lashes charred,
Their blackened teeth set firm and hard.

Their mad assailants rave and reel,
And face, as men who scorn to feel,
The close-lined, three-edged prongs of steel,

[113]

Till faintness follows closing-in,
When, faltering headlong down, they spin
Like leaves. But those pay well who win Albuera.

Out of six thousands souls that sware
To hold the mount, or pass elsewhere,
But eighteen hundred muster there.

Pale Colonels, Captains, ranksmen lie,
Facing the earth or facing sky;—
They strove to live, they stretch to die.

Friends, foemen, mingle; heap and heap.—
Hide their hacked bones, Earth!—Deep, deep, deep,
Where harmless worms caress and creep.

Hide their hacked bones, Earth!—deep, deep, deep,
Where harmless worms caress and creep.—
What man can grieve? what woman weep?
Better than waking is to sleep! Albuera!

BEFORE WATERLOO

Yes, the coneys are scared by the thud of hoofs,
And their white scuts flash at their vanishing heels,
And swallows abandon the hamlet-roofs.

The mole's tunnelled chambers are crushed by wheels,
The lark's eggs scattered, their owners fled;
And the hedgehog's household the sapper unseals.

[114]

The snail draws in that terrible tread,
But in vain; he is crushed by the felloe-rim;
The worm asks what can be overhead,

And wriggles deep from a scene so grim,
And guesses him safe; for he does not know
What a foul red flood will be soaking him!

Beaten about by the heel and toe
Are butterflies, sick of the day's long rheum,
To die of a worse than the weather-foe.

Trodden and bruised to a miry tomb
Are ears that have greened but will never be gold,
And flowers in the blood that will never bloom.

Thomas Hardy

THE SOLDIER

Yes. Why do we all, seeing of a soldier, bless him? bless
Our redcoats, our tars? Both these being, the greater part,
But frail clay, nay but foul clay. Here it is: the heart,
Since, proud, it calls the calling manly, gives a guess
That, hopes that, makesbelieve, the men must be no less;
It fancies, feigns, deems, dears the artist after his art;
And fain will find as sterling all as all is smart,
And scarlet wear the spirit of war there express.

Mark Christ our King. He knows war, served his soldiering
    through;

[115]

He of all can handle a rope best. There he bides in bliss
Now, and seeing somewhere some man do all that man can do,
For love he leans forth, needs his neck must fall on, kiss,
And cry 'O Christ-done deed! So God-made-flesh does too:
Were I come o'er again' cries Christ 'it should be this.'

GERARD MANLEY HOPKINS

DEATH IN THE CORN

AMONG poppies in a field of maize
lies a soldier, still unfound,
two nights already and two days,
with his grievous wounds unbound.

Wild with fever, parched with thirst,
in the throes of death he tries
to lift his head—one vision first—
then upward roll his blood-shot eyes.

Through the grain the scythe-blades hum,
he sees his town on a harvest-dawn.
Farewell, farewell, my world of home—
and the head sinks and he is gone.

DETLEV VON LILIENCRON
Translated by C. F. MacIntyre

THE SLEEPER IN THE VALLEY

THROUGH a green gorge the river like a fountain
Sings, while the rags of grass that hang upon
Its silver banks, this side of the proud mountain,
Blaze: a little valley absorbs the sun.

A soldier, young, his head not covered up,
Is bathed in fresh blue water-cress—and dreams?
His lips are parted; under the sky's cup
He lies in his green bed where the light streams.

His feet in gladiolas, he seems to smile
Like a sick child who fitfully naps a while:
Nature, rock him tenderly, he is cold!

Sweet odors do not make his nostrils tremble;
The noon siesta, hand on breast, resemble
Peace: in his right side there are two red holes.

ARTHUR RIMBAUD
Translated by S. R.

SONNET

("... Frenchmen of '70, Bonapartists or Republicans,
remember your forefathers of '92 ..."—Paul de Cas-
sagnac, in *Le Pays)*

DEAD men of 'ninety-two, also of 'ninety-three,
Pale at the lusty kiss of liberty, who broke

Resolvedly beneath your clogs the tyrants' yoke
That bows the soul and head of all humanity;

Men who enjoyed ecstatic glory in your pain,
Whose hearts beneath your tatters leapt with love alone
O soldiers whom your noble lover Death has sown
That in the ancient furrows you may rise again;

Whose blood washed greatness clean of all impurity,
Dead of Valmy, Fleurus, dead men of Italy,
You million murdered Christs, your eyes sombre and true;

You and the French Republic we consigned to sleep,
We whom the blows of Kings in prostrate bondage keep—
And these de Cassagnacs speak to us now of you!

ARTHUR RIMBAUD
Translated by Norman Cameron

EVIL

WHILST the red spittle of the grape-shot sings
All day across the endless sky, and whilst entire
Battalions, green or scarlet, rallied by their kings,
Disintegrate in crumpled masses under fire;

Whilst an abominable madness seeks to pound
A hundred thousand men into a smoking mess—
Pitiful dead in summer grass, on the rich ground
Out of which Nature wrought these men in holiness;

[118]

He is a God who sees it all, and laughs aloud
At damask altar-cloths, incense and chalices,
Who falls asleep lulled by adoring liturgies

And wakens when some mother, in her anguish bowed
And weeping till her old black bonnet shakes with grief
Offers him a big sou wrapped in her handkerchief.

ARTHUR RIMBAUD
Translated by Norman Cameron

EPITAPH ON AN ARMY
OF MERCENARIES

THESE, in the day when heaven was falling,
    The hour when earth's foundations fled,
Followed their mercenary calling
    And took their wages and are dead.

Their shoulders held the sky suspended;
    They stood, and earth's foundations stay;
What God abandoned, these defended,
    And saved the sum of things for pay.

A. E. HOUSMAN

THE DAY OF BATTLE

"FAR I hear the bugle blow
To call me where I would not go,

[119]

And the guns begin the song,
'Soldier fly or stay for long.'

"Comrade, if to turn and fly
Made a soldier never die,
Fly I would, for who would not?
'Tis sure no pleasure to be shot.

"But since the man that runs away
Lives to die another day,
And cowards' funerals, when they come,
Are not wept so well at home,

"Therefore, though the best is bad,
Stand and do the best, my lad;
Stand and fight and see your slain,
And take the bullet in your brain."

A. E. Housman

DANNY DEEVER

'What are the bugles blowin' for?' said Files-on-Parade.
'To turn you out, to turn you out,' the Colour-Sergeant said.
'What makes you look so white, so white?' said Files-on-Parade.
'I'm dreadin' what I've got to watch,' the Colour-Sergeant said.
   For they're hangin' Danny Deever, you can hear the Dead
      March play,
   The regiment's in 'ollow square—they're hangin' him today;

They've taken of his buttons off an' cut his stripes away,
An' they're hangin' Danny Deever in the mornin'.

'What makes the rear-rank breathe so 'ard?' said Files-on-
Parade.
'It's bitter cold, it's bitter cold,' the Colour-Sergeant said.
'What makes that front-rank man fall down?' says Files-on-
Parade.
'A touch o' sun, a touch o' sun,' the Colour-Sergeant said.
They are hangin' Danny Deever, they are marchin' of 'im
round,
They 'ave 'alted Danny Deever by 'is coffin on the ground;
An' 'e'll swing in 'arf a minute for a sneakin' shootin' hound—
O they're hangin' Danny Deever in the mornin'.

' 'Is cot was right-'and cot to mine,' said Files-on-Parade.
' 'E's sleepin' out and far to-night,' the Colour-Sergeant said.
'I've drunk 'is beer a score o' times,' said Files-on-Parade.
' 'E's drinkin' bitter beer alone,' the Colour-Sergeant said.
They are hangin' Danny Deever, you must mark 'im to 'is
place,
For 'e shot a comrade sleepin'—you must look 'im in the
face;
Nine-'undred of 'is county an' the regiment's disgrace,
While they're hangin' Danny Deever in the mornin'.

'What's that so black agin the sun?' said Files-on-Parade.
'It's Danny fightin' 'ard for life,' the Colour-Sergeant said.
'What's that that whimpers over-'ead?' said Files-on-Parade.
'It's Danny's soul that's passin' now,' the Colour-Sergeant said.
For they're done with Danny Deever, you can 'ear the quick-
step play,

The regiment's in column, an' they're marchin' us away;
Ho! the young recruits are shakin' an' they'll want their beer
    today
After hangin' Danny Deever in the mornin'.

                                        RUDYARD KIPLING

WAR IS KIND

Do NOT weep, maiden, for war is kind.
Because your lover threw wild hands toward the sky
And the affrighted steed ran on alone,
Do not weep.
War is kind.

        Hoarse, booming drums of the regiment,
        Little souls who thirst for fight,
        These men were born to drill and die.
        The unexplained glory flies above them,
        Great is the battle-god, great, and his kingdom—
        A field where a thousand corpses lie.

Do not weep, babe, for war is kind.
Because your father tumbled in the yellow trenches,
Raged at his breast, gulped and died,
Do not weep.
War is kind.

        Swift blazing flag of the regiment,
        Eagle with crest of red and gold,
        These men were born to drill and die.
        Point for them the virtue of slaughter,

Make plain to them the excellence of killing
And a field where a thousand corpses lie.

Mother, whose heart hung humble as a button
On the bright, splendid shroud of your son,
Do not weep.
War is kind.

STEPHEN CRANE

CAESAR

CAESAR, serene Caesar, your foot on all,
The hard fists in the beard, and the gloomy eyes
Pregnant with eagles and battles of foreseen fall,
Your heart swells, feeling itself omnipotent cause.

In vain the lake trembles, licking its rosy bed,
Vainly glistens the gold of the young wheat straws.
You harden in the knots of your gathered body
The word which must finally rive your tight-clenched jaws.

The spacious world, beyond the immense horizon,
The Empire awaits the torch, the order, the lightning
Which will turn the evening to a furious dawn.

Happily there on the waves, and cradled in hazard,
A lazy fisherman is drifting and singing,
Not knowing what thunder collects in the center of Caesar.

PAUL VALÉRY
Translated by C. F. MacIntyre

[123]

THE SCYTHIANS

You are the millions, we are multitude
And multitude and multitude.
Come, fight! Yea, we are Scythians,
Yea, Asians, a squint-eyed, greedy brood.

For you—the centuries, for us—one hour,
Like slaves, obeying and abhorred,
We were the shield between the breeds
Of Europe and the raging Mongol horde.

For centuries the hammers on your forge
Drowned out the avalanche's boom;
You heard like wild, fantastic tales
Old Lisbon's and Messina's sudden doom.

Yea, you have long since ceased to love
As our hot blood can love; the taste
You have forgotten, of a love
That burns like fire and like fire lays waste.

All things we love: cold numbers' burning chill,
The ecstasies that secret bloom.
All things we know: the Gallic light
And the parturient Germanic gloom.

And we remember all: Parisian hells,
The breath of Venice's lagoons,
Far fragrance of green lemon groves,
And dim Cologne's cathedral-splintered moons.

[124]

And flesh we love, its color and its taste,
Its deathy odor, heavy, raw.
And is it our guilt if your bones
May crack beneath our powerful supple paw?

It is our wont to seize wild colts at play:
They rear and impotently shake
Wild manes—we crush their mighty croups.
And shrewish women slaves we tame—or break.

Come unto us, from the black ways of war,
Come to our peaceful arms and rest.
Comrades, while it is not too late,
Sheathe the old sword. May brotherhood be blest.

If not, we have not anything to lose.
We also know old perfidies.
By sick descendants you will be
Accursed for centuries and centuries.

To welcome pretty Europe, we shall spread
And scatter in the tangled space
Of our wild thickets. We shall turn
To you our alien Asiatic face.

For centuries your eyes were toward the East.
Our pearls you hoarded in your chests,
And mockingly you bode the day
When you could aim your cannon at our breasts.

The time has come. Disaster beats its wings.
With every day the insults grow.
The hour will strike, and without ruth
Your proud and powerless Paestums be laid low.

Oh, pause, old world, while life still beats in you,
Oh, weary one, oh, worn, oh, wise!
Halt here, as once did Oedipus
Before the Sphinx's enigmatic eyes.

Yea, Russia is a Sphinx. Exulting, grieving,
And sweating blood, she cannot sate
Her eyes that gaze and gaze and gaze
At you with stone-lipped love for you, and hate.

Go, all of you, to Ural fastnesses.
We clear the ground for the appalling scenes
Of war between the savage Mongol hordes
And pitiless science with its massed machines.

But we, we shall no longer be your shield.
But, careless of the battle-cries,
Will watch the deadly duel seethe,
Aloof, with indurate and narrow eyes.

We will not move when the ferocious Hun
Despoils the corpse and leaves it bare,
Burns towns, herds cattle in the church,
And smell of white flesh roasting fills the air.

For the last time, old world, we bid you come,
Feast brotherly within our walls.
To share our peace and glowing toil
Once only the barbarian lyre calls.

ALEKSANDR BLOK
*Translated by Babette Deutsch
and Avrahm Yarmolinsky*

PART THREE

JOHNNY, I HARDLY KNEW YE

WHILE going the road to sweet Athy,
  Hurroo! Hurroo!
While going the road to sweet Athy,
  Hurroo! Hurroo!
While going the road to sweet Athy,
A stick in my hand and a drop in my eye,
A doleful damsel I heard cry:—
  'Och, Johnny, I hardly knew ye!
With drums and guns, and guns and drums
  The enemy nearly slew ye,
   My darling dear, you look so queer,
  Och, Johnny, I hardly knew ye!

'Where are your eyes that looked so mild?
  Hurroo! Hurroo!
Where are your eyes that looked so mild?
  Hurroo! Hurroo!
When my poor heart you first beguiled?
Why did you run from me and the child?
  Och, Johnny, I hardly knew ye!
With drums, &c.

'Where are the legs with which you run?
  Hurroo! Hurroo!
Where are the legs with which you run?
  Hurroo! Hurroo!
'Where are the legs with which you run?
When you went to carry a gun?—
Indeed your dancing days are done!

Och, Johnny, I hardly knew ye!
With drums, &c.

'It grieved my heart to see you sail,
    Hurroo! Hurroo!
It grieved my heart to see you sail,
    Hurroo! Hurroo!
It grieved my heart to see you sail
Though from my heart you took leg bail,—
Like a cod you're doubled up head and tail.
    Och, Johnny, I hardly knew ye!
With drums, &c.

'You haven't an arm and you haven't a leg,
    Hurroo! Hurroo!
You haven't an arm and you haven't a leg,
    Hurroo! Hurroo!
You haven't an arm and you haven't a leg.
You're an eyeless, noseless, chickenless egg;
You'll have to be put in a bowl to beg;
    Och, Johnny, I hardly knew ye!
With drums, &c.

'I'm happy for to see you home,
    Hurroo! Hurroo!
I'm happy for to see you home,
    Hurroo! Hurroo!
I'm happy for to see you home,
All from the island of Sulloon,
So low in flesh, so high in bone,
    Och, Johnny, I hardly knew ye!
With drums, &c.

[129]

'But sad as it is to see you so,
  Hurroo! Hurroo!
But sad as it to see you so,
  Hurroo! Hurroo!
But sad as it is to see you so,
And to think of you now as an object of woe,
Your Peggy'll still keep ye on as her beau;
  Och. Johnny, I hardly knew ye!
With drums and guns, and guns and drums
  The enemy nearly slew ye,
  My darling dear, you look so queer,
  Och, Johnny, I hardly knew ye!'

ANONYMOUS

AN IRISH AIRMAN FORESEES
HIS DEATH

I KNOW that I shall meet my fate
Somewhere among the clouds above;
Those that I fight I do not hate,
Those that I guard I do not love;
My country is Kiltartan Cross,
My countrymen Kiltartan's poor,
No likely end could bring them less
Or leave them happier than before.
Nor law, nor duty bade me fight,
Nor public men, nor cheering crowds,
A lonely impulse of delight
Drove to this tumult in the clouds;
I balanced all, brought all to mind,

[130]

The years to come seemed waste of breath,
A waste of breath the years behind
In balance with this life, this death.

WILLIAM BUTLER YEATS

TO A YOUNG LEADER OF THE FIRST WORLD WAR

NOT as you had dreamed was the battle's issue . . .
When the broken army yielded up its weapons
You stood with me, sad, as when, after feasting
The sober work begins, stripped of its honors . . .
Tears welled from your eyes, for the wasted treasure
Of crucial years.

Do not, however, ape the unthinking masses
Who acclaim today and discard tomorrow,
Who smash the landmark over which they stumbled . . .
Sudden rise, right up to the gate of victory,
Plunge, in oppression—both contain a meaning
That lies in you.

All to which you grew through the glorious struggle
Stays with you untouched, steels for future dins . . .
See, as you looked up, walking with me slowly,
The shine of the sunset around your flaming
Hair become a ring first of rays around you
And than a crown.

STEFAN GEORGE
Translated by E. B. Ashton

[131]

PRELUDE XXIII

WE ARE those same children who amazed
before your lordly stride but not afraid
assemble when a warrior's trumpet brays
that in open field your flag is raised.

We come to stand at our stern master's side
who passes in review his men of war
no weeping turns us from our guiding star
no arms of friends nor kisses of a bride.

And we are happy reading from his eyes
what shining dreams foretell us of our doom
though honor or dark fortune be the prize
of his turned-down or his uplifted thumb.

What glorifies us makes us glad and free
we take from his hand as our wage, our faith
and pride are strong and when he signals we
are ready to follow him to night or death.

STEFAN GEORGE
Translated by C. F. MacIntyre

HAPPY ARE THOSE WHO HAVE DIED

HAPPY they who die for the earth which also dies
But only that it was in a just war.
Happy they who died for the four corners of the earth.
Happy they who have died by a death that is august.

[132]

Happy they who have died in great battles,
Lying upon the ground facing God.
Happy those who have died in a last stand
Among all the trappings of great funeral ceremonies.

Happy they who have died for carnal cities.
For they are the body of the city of God.
Happy are they who have died for their hearth and their fire
And the pitiful honor of their ancestral mansions.

For these things are the picture and the beginning
And the first work and the testing of the house of God.
Happy are those who have died in this encirclement,
In the tight clasp of honor and the earthly avowal.

For this confession of honor is the beginning
And the first attempt at an eternal confession.
Happy are those who have died in this prostration,
In the accomplishment of this earthly vow.

For their consecration of earth is the beginning
And the first trial of a faith.
Happy are those who have died in this coronation
And this obéisance and this humility.

Happy are those who have died, for they come back
In the first piece of the rooftree and the first sod.
Happy are those who have died in a just war.
Happy the ripe stalks and the harvested grain.

Charles Péguy
Translated by Jessie Degen and R. E.

THEY WENT FORTH TO BATTLE
BUT THEY ALWAYS FELL

They went forth to battle but they always fell;
   Their eyes were fixed above the sullen shields;
Nobly they fought and bravely but not well,
And sank, heart-wounded by a subtle spell.
   They knew not fear that to the foeman yields,
   They were not weak, as one who vainly wields
A futile weapon; yet the sad scrolls tell
How on the hard-fought field they always fell.

It was a secret music that they heard,
   A sad sweet plea for pity and for peace;
And that which pierced the heart was but a word,
Though the white breast was red-lipped where the sword
   Pierced a fierce cruel kiss, to put surcease
   On its hot thirst, but drank a hot increase.
Ah, they by some strange troubling doubt were stirred,
And died for hearing what no foeman heard.

They went forth to battle but they always fell;
   Their might was not the might of lifted spears;
Over the battle clamor came a spell
Of troubling music, and they fought not well.
   Their wreaths are willows and their tribute, tears;
   Their names are old sad stories in men's ears;
Yet they will scatter the red hordes of Hell,
Who went to battle forth and always fell.

Shaemas O'Sheel

THE LAST EVENING

NIGHT and the distant rumbling; for the train
of the whole army passed by the estate.
But still he raised his eyes and played again
the clavichord and gazed at her . . . and waited

almost like a man looking in a mirror
which was completely filled with his young face,
knowing how his features bore his sorrow,
more beautifully seductive with the grace

of music. The scene faded out. Instead,
wearily at the window, in her trouble,
she held the violent thumping of her heart.

He finished. The dawn wind was blowing hard.
And strangely alien on the mirror table
stood the black shako with its white death's-head.

RAINER MARIA RILKE
Translated by C. F. MacIntyre

A SOLDIER

HE IS that fallen lance that lies as hurled,
That lies unlifted now, come dew, come rust,
But still lies pointed as it plowed the dust.
If we who sight along it round the world,
See nothing worthy to have been its mark,

[135]

It is because like men we look too near,
Forgetting that as fitted to the sphere,
Our missiles always make too short an arc.
They fall, they rip the grass, they intersect
The curve of earth, and striking, break their own;
They make us cringe for metal-point on stone.
But this we know, the obstacle that checked
And tripped the body, shot the spirit on
Further than target ever showed or stone.

ROBERT FROST

GRASS

PILE the bodies high at Austerlitz and Waterloo.
Shovel them under and let me work—
      I am the grass; I cover all.

And pile them high at Gettysburg
And pile them high at Ypres and Verdun.
Shovel them under and let me work.
Two years, ten years, and passengers ask the conductor:

      What place is this?
      Where are we now?

      I am the grass.
      Let me work.

CARL SANDBURG

A. E. F.

THERE will be a rusty gun on the wall, sweetheart,
The rifle grooves curling with flakes of rust.
A spider will make a silver string nest in the darkest, warmest
    corner of it.
The trigger and the range-finder, they too will be rusty.
And no hands will polish the gun, and it will hang on the wall.
Forefingers and thumbs will point absently and casually to-
    ward it.
It will be spoken among half-forgotten, wished-to-be-forgotten
    things.
They will tell the spider: Go on, you're doing good work.

CARL SANDBURG

WAR

MAIN artery of fighting
        Contact by hearing
Where one aims in the direction "of noises heard"
        The youths of the 1915 class
And those electrified wires
Do not weep then over the horrors of war
Before it we had only the surface
Of the earth and of the seas
After it we shall have the abysses
The substratum and the whole space of aviation
Masters of direction
Afterwards afterwards
We shall take all the joys

[137]

Of the conquerors who let themselves go
Women Sports Work Shops Commerce
Fire Crystal Swiftness
Voice Look Touch aside
And together in the touch come from far away
From still farther away
From the Beyond of this earth

GUILLAUME APOLLINAIRE

Translated by Jessie Degen and R. E.

SHADOW

THERE you are once more near me
Memories of my friends dead in the war
The olive branch of time
Memories which make only one
As a hundred skins of fur make only one cloth
And those thousands of wounds make only one newspaper
    article
Apparition impalpable and shadowy which has taken
The changing form of my shadow
An Indian in ambush through eternity
Shadow, you climb up close to me
But you do not hear me any more
You will never know the heavenly poems that I sing
While I, I hear you and I see you still
Destinies
Multiple shadow which the sunshine keeps you
You who love me enough never to leave me
And who dance in the sunshine without making any dust

Inky shadow of the sunshine
Handwriting of my light
Caisson of regrets
A god humbled

GUILLAUME APOLLINAIRE
Translated by Jessie Degen and R. E.

THESE FOUGHT IN ANY CASE

from ODE POUR L'ELECTION DE SON SEPULCHRE

THESE fought in any case,
and some believing, pro domo, in any case . . .

Some quick to arm,
some for adventure,
some from fear of weakness,
some from fear of censure
some for love of slaughter, in imagination,
learning later . . .

Some in fear, learning love of slaughter;
died some, pro patria, non 'dulce' non 'et decor' . . .
walked eye-deep in hell
believing in old men's lies, then unbelieving
came home, home to a lie,
home to many deceits,
home to old lies and new infamy;
usury age-old and age-thick
and liars in public places.

[139]

Daring as never before, wastage as never before.
Young blood and high blood,
fair cheeks, and fine bodies;

fortitude as never before

frankness as never before,
disillusions as never told in the old days,
hysterias, trench confessions,
laughter out of dead bellies.

           ❀   ❀   ❀

There died a myriad,
And of the best, among them,
For an old bitch gone in the teeth,
For a botched civilization,

Charm, smiling at the good mouth,
Quick eyes gone under earth's lid,

For two gross of broken statues,
For a few thousand battered books.

EZRA POUND

HOW COULD WE, BEFOREHAND, LIVE IN QUIET

How could we, beforehand, live in quiet,
Neither harm nor gladness waiting for;
Dream not of the fiery dawn of riot,
Of the triumph-trumpet's sounding roar.

How could we—the time is not yet spent.
See on us the sun of spirit rise;
Stern, the spirit's sun, beneficent,
Fill and overflow our native skies.

In the endless steppes, the savage magic,
In the forest thicket, secret, still,
There is nothing torturing or tragic
For the soul, or bitter for the will.

Lo, I feel the breath of autumn weather,
Labors of the sun shall end—I see
All the season's fruit the folk shall gather,
Ripe and golden, from the spirit's tree.

NIKOLAI GUMILEV
Translated by Jeannette Eyre

THE DUG-OUT

WHY do you lie with your legs ungainly huddled,
And one arm bent across your sullen cold
Exhausted face? It hurts my heart to watch you,
Deep-shadow'd from the candle's guttering gold:
And you wonder why I shake you by the shoulder;
Drowsy, you mumble and sigh and shift your head . . .
You are too young to fall asleep for ever;
And when you sleep you remind me of the dead.
1918

SIEGFRIED SASSOON

[141]

INTO BATTLE

THE naked earth is warm with spring,
  And with green grass and bursting trees
Leans to the sun's gaze glorying,
  And quivers in the sunny breeze;
And life is colour and warmth and light
  And a striving evermore for these;
And he is dead who will not fight;
  And who dies fighting has increase.

The fighting man shall from the sun
  Take warmth, and life from the glowing earth;
Speed with the light-foot winds to run,
  And with the trees to newer birth;
And find, when fighting shall be done,
  Great rest, and fullness after dearth.

All the bright company of Heaven
  Hold him in their high comradeship,
The Dog-Star, and the Sisters Seven,
  Orion's Belt and sworded hip.

The woodland trees that stand together,
  They stand to him each one a friend;
They gently speak in the windy weather;
  They guide to valley and ridge's end.

The kestrel hovering by day,
  And the little owls that call by night,
Bid him be swift and keen as they,
  As keen of ear, as swift of sight.

[142]

The blackbird sings to him, 'Brother, brother,
  If this be the last song you shall sing,
Sing well, for you may not sing another;
  Brother, sing.'

In dreary, doubtful, waiting hours,
  Before the brazen frenzy starts,
The horses show him nobler powers;
  O patient eyes, courageous hearts!

And when the burning moment breaks,
  And all things else are out of mind,
And only joy of battle takes
  Him by the throat, and makes him blind,

Through joy and blindness he shall know,
  Not caring much to know, that still
Nor lead nor steel shall reach him, so
  That it be not the Destin'd Will.

The thundering line of battle stands,
  And in the air Death moans and sings;
But Day shall clasp him with strong hands,
  And Night shall fold him in soft wings.

JULIAN GRENFELL

TRIUMPHAL MARCH

from CORIOLAN

STONE, bronze, stone, steel, stone, oakleaves, horses' heels
Over the paving.
And the flags. And the trumpets. And so many eagles.
How many? Count them. And such a press of people.
We hardly knew ourselves that day, or knew the City.
This is the way to the temple, and we so many crowding the
    way.
So many waiting, how many waiting? what did it matter, on
    such a day?
Are they coming? No, not yet. You can see some eagles. And
    hear the trumpets.
Here they come. Is he coming?
The natural wakeful life of our Ego is a perceiving.
We can wait with our stools and our sausages.
Who comes first? Can you see? Tell us. It is

> 5,800,000 rifles and carbines,
> 102,000 machine guns,
> 28,000 trench mortars,
> 53,000 field and heavy guns,

I cannot tell how many projectiles, mines and fuses,

> 13,000 aeroplanes,
> 24,000 aeroplane engines,
> 50,000 ammunition waggons,
> now 55,000 army waggons,
> 11,000 field kitchens,
> 1,150 field bakeries.

[144]

What a time that took. Will it be he now? No
Those are the golf club Captains, these the Scouts,
And now the *société gymnastique de Poissy*
And now come the Mayor and the Liverymen. Look
There he is now, look:
There is no interrogation in his eyes
Or in the hands, quiet over the horse's neck,
And the eyes watchful, waiting, perceiving, indifferent.
O hidden under the dove's wing, hidden in the turtle's breast,
Under the palmtree at noon, under the running water
At the still point of the turning world. O hidden.

Now they go up to the temple. Then the sacrifice.
Now come the virgins bearing urns, urns containing
Dust
Dust
Dust of dust, and now
Stone, bronze, stone, steel, stone, oakleaves, horses' heels
Over the paving.

That is all we could see. But how many eagles! and how many
        trumpets!
(And Easter Day, we didn't get to the country,
So we took young Cyril to church. And they rang a bell
And he said right out loud, *crumpets.*)
                        Don't throw away that sausage,
It'll come in handy. He's artful. Please, will you give us a light?
Light
Light
Et les soldats faisaient la haie? ILS LA FAISAIENT.

                                          T. S. ELIOT

[145]

RETURNING, WE HEAR THE LARKS

Sombre the night is:
And, though we have our lives, we know
What sinister threat lurks there.

Dragging these anguished limbs, we only know
This poison-blasted track opens on our camp—
On a little safe sleep.

But hark! Joy—joy—strange joy.
Lo! Heights of night ringing with unseen larks:
Music showering on our upturned listening faces.

Death could drop from the dark
As easily as song—
But song only dropped,
Like a blind man's dreams on the sand
By dangerous tides;
Like a girl's dark hair, for she dreams no ruin lies there,
Or her kisses where a serpent hides.

Isaac Rosenberg

BREAK OF DAY IN THE TRENCHES

The darkness crumbles away—
It is the same old druid Time as ever.
Only a live thing leaps my hand—
A queer sardonic rat—

[146]

As I pull the parapet's poppy
To stick behind my ear.
Droll rat, they would shoot you if they knew
Your cosmopolitan sympathies
(And God knows what antipathies).
Now you have touched this English hand
You will do the same to a German—
Soon, no doubt, if it be your pleasure
To cross the sleeping green between.
It seems you inwardly grin as you pass
Strong eyes, fine limbs, haughty athletes
Less chanced than you for life,
Bonds to the whims of murder,
Sprawled in the bowels of the earth,
The torn fields of France.
What do you see in our eyes
At the shrieking iron and flame
Hurled through still heavens?
What quaver—what heart aghast?
Poppies whose roots are in man's veins
Drop, and are ever dropping;
But mine in my ear is safe,
Just a little white with the dust.

ISAAC ROSENBERG

OUR CHILDREN'S CHILDREN
WILL MARVEL

Our children's children will marvel,
Leafing the textbook:
" 'Fourteen—'Seventeen—'Nineteen.

[147]

How did they live? Poor souls—poor devils!"
Children of a new age will read of battles,
Memorize the names of leaders, orators,
The numbers of the slain,
And dates;
They will not learn how sweet, on the field of battle, roses
    smelled,
How clear, amid the cannons' voices, rang the chirping of
    martins,
The beauty in those years that was
Life.
Never, never laughed the sun with joy
As on the city laid in ruins,
When people, crawling out of cellars,
Cried out in wonder: "There is still a sun!"
Insurgent speeches thundered,
Zealous troops perished,
But the soldiers learned how snowdrops can smell
The hour before the attack.
They led men out in the morning, shot them down,
But they, only they knew what April morning means.
In the slanting rays the cupolas flamed,
But the wind prayed, "Wait, a minute! a minute more!"
They kissed, and could not tear themselves from the sad lips,
Nor did they loose the tightly clasped hands;
They loved—I shall die! I shall die!
They loved—burn, flame, on the wind!
They loved—O where, say where you are!
They loved, as men can love only here, on a troubled and ten-
    der star.
In those years there were no gardens of golden fruits,
But only the instant's flower, one doomed May;
In those years there was no "au revoir,"

[148]

Only a sounding, short "good-bye."
Read about us—marvel!
Sorrow—you did not live with us!
Guests of earth, we came for one sole evening.
We loved, we destroyed, in our hour of death we lived.
But above us stood the eternal stars,
And beneath them you were conceived.
In your eyes our longing still smoulders,
In your speeches our revolt still rages.
Far scattered we in the night and the ages, the ages,
The quenched sparks of our life.

Kiev, 1919

ILYA EHRENBURG
Translated by Jeannette Eyre

GREATER LOVE

RED lips are not so red
    As the stained stones kissed by the English dead.
Kindness of wooed and wooer
Seems shame to their love pure.
O Love, your eyes lose lure
    When I behold eyes blinded in my stead!

Your slender attitude
    Trembles not exquisite like limbs knife-skewed,
Rolling and rolling there
Where God seems not to care;
Till the fierce Love they bear
    Cramps them in death's extreme decrepitude.

[149]

Your voice sings not so soft,—
    Though even as wind murmuring through raftered loft,—
Your dear voice is not dear,
Gentle, and evening clear,
As theirs whom none now hear,
    Now earth has stopped their piteous mouths that coughed.

Heart, you were never hot,
    Nor large, nor full like hearts made great with shot;
And though your hand be pale,
Paler are all which trail
Your cross through flame and hail:
    Weep, you may weep, for you may touch them not.

WILFRED OWEN

THE SHOW

    We have fallen in the dreams the ever-living
    Breathe on the tarnished mirror of the world,
    And then smooth out with ivory hands and sigh

W. B. YEATS

MY SOUL looked down from a vague height with Death,
As unremembering how I rose or why,
And saw a sad land, weak with sweats of dearth,
Gray, cratered like the moon with hollow woe,
And pitted with great pocks and scabs of plagues.

Across its beard, that horror of harsh wire,
There moved thin caterpillars, slowly uncoiled.

[150]

It seemed they pushed themselves to be as plugs
Of ditches, where they writhed and shrivelled, killed.

By them had slimy paths been trailed and scraped
Round myriad warts that might be little hills.

From gloom's last dregs these long-strung creatures crept,
And vanished out of dawn down hidden holes.

(And smell came up from those foul openings
As out of mouths, or deep wounds deepening.)

On dithering feet upgathered, more and more,
Brown strings, towards strings of gray, with bristling spines,
All migrants from green fields, intent on mire.

Those that were gray, of more abundant spawns,
Ramped on the rest and ate them and were eaten.

I saw their bitten backs curve, loop, and straighten
I watched those agonies curl, lift, and flatten.

Whereat, in terror what that sight might mean,
I reeled and shivered earthward like a feather.

And Death fell with me, like a deepening moan.
And He, picking a manner of worm, which half had hid
Its bruises in the earth, but crawled no further,
Showed me its feet, the feet of many men,
And the fresh-severed head of it, my head.

WILFRED OWEN

[151]

STRANGE MEETING

I<small>T SEEMED</small> that out of battle I escaped
Down some profound dull tunnel, long since scooped
Through granites which titanic wars had groined.
Yet also there encumbered sleepers groaned,
Too fast in thought or death to be bestirred.
Then, as I probed them, one sprang up, and stared
With piteous recognition in fixed eyes,
Lifting distressful hands as if to bless.
And by his smile, I knew that sullen hall,
By his dead smile I knew we stood in Hell.
With a thousand pains that vision's face was grained;
Yet no blood reached there from the upper ground,
And no guns thumped, or down the flues made moan.
'Strange friend,' I said, 'here is no cause to mourn.'
'None,' said the other, 'save the undone years,
The hopelessness. Whatever hope is yours,
Was my life also; I went hunting wild
After the wildest beauty in the world,
Which lies not calm in eyes, or braided hair,
But mocks the steady running of the hour,
And if it grieves, grieves richlier than here.
For by my glee might many men have laughed,
And of my weeping something had been left,
Which must die now. I mean the truth untold,
The pity of war, the pity war distilled.
Now men will go content with what we spoiled.
Or, discontent, boil bloody, and be spilled.
They will be swift with swiftness of the tigress,
None will break ranks, though nations trek from progress.
Courage was mine, and I had mystery,

Wisdom was mine, and I had mastery;
To miss the march of this retreating world
Into vain citadels that are not walled.
Then, when much blood had clogged their chariot-wheels
I would go up and wash them from sweet wells,
Even with truths that lie too deep for taint.
I would have poured my spirit without stint
But not through wounds; not on the cess of war.
Foreheads of men have bled where no wounds were.
I am the enemy you killed, my friend.
I knew you in this dark; for so you frowned
Yesterday through me as you jabbed and killed.
I parried; but my hands were loath and cold.
Let us sleep now . . .'

WILFRED OWEN

"MY SWEET OLD ETCETERA"

    my sweet old etcetera
    aunt lucy during the recent

    war could and what
    is more did tell you just
    what everybody was fighting

    for,
    my sister

    isabel created hundreds
    (and

[153]

hundreds) of socks not to
mention shirts fleaproof earwarmers

etcetera wristers etcetera, my
mother hoped that

i would die etcetera
bravely of course my father used
to become hoarse talking about how it was
a privilege and if only he
could meanwhile my

self etcetera lay quietly
in the deep mud et
cetera
(dreaming,
et
    cetera, of
Your smile
eyes knees and of your Etcetera)

E. E. Cummings

"NEXT TO OF COURSE GOD AMERICA"

"next to of course god america i
love you land of the pilgrims' and so forth oh
say can you see by the dawn's early my
country 'tis of centuries come and go
and are no more what of it we should worry

in every language even deafanddumb
thy sons acclaim your glorious name by gorry
by jingo by gee by gosh by gum
why talk of beauty what could be more beaut-
iful than these heroic happy dead
who rushed like lions to the roaring slaughter
they did not stop to think they died instead
then shall the voice of liberty be mute?"

He spoke. And drank rapidly a glass of water

                                    E. E. CUMMINGS

"LISTEN"

          lis
          -ten

          you know what i mean when
          the first guy drops you know
          everybody feels sick or
          when they throw in a few gas
          and the oh baby shrapnel
          or my feet getting dim freezing or
          up to your you know what in water or
          with the bugs crawling right all up
          all everywhere over you all me everyone
          that's-been there knows what
          i mean a god damned lot of
          people don't and never
          never

                    [155]

will know,
they don't want

to
no

ON THIS MY SICK-BED BEATS THE WORLD

On this my sick-bed beats the world
Through bandages alarm is tearing at my mind.
My brothers go to fight for liberty,
My brothers go to fight, and no one stays behind.

On this my sick-bed beats the world,
But also death is breathing on it in this darkened hall . . .
Why can I not go with you, brothers?
Why must I die when I had hoped to fall?

Jiří Wolker
Translated by Karl W. Deutsch

EPITAPH

Here lies the poet Wolker, lover of the world,
Who for its greater justice fought and sung;
Ere he his heart had fully yet unfurled
He died. Was twenty-four years young.

Jiří Wolker
Translated by Karl W. Deutsch

[156]

PART FOUR

THE SOLDIER'S WOUND

How red the rose that is the soldier's wound,
The wounds of many soldiers, the wounds of all
The soldiers that have fallen, red in blood,
The soldier of time grown deathless in great size.

A mountain in which no ease is ever found,
Unless indifference to deeper death
Is ease, stands in the dark, a shadow's hill,
And there the soldier of time has deathless rest.

Concentric circles of shadows, motionless
Of their own part, yet moving on the wind,
Form metaphysical convolutions in the sleep
Of time's red soldier deathless on his bed.

The shadows of his fellows ring him round
In the high night, the summer breathes for them
Its fragrance, a heavy somnolence, and for him,
For the soldier of time, it breathes a summer sleep,

In which his wound is good because life was.
No part of him was ever part of death.
A woman smoothes her forehead with her hand
And the soldier of time lies calm beneath that stroke.

WALLACE STEVENS

THE WARS and THE UNKNOWN SOLDIER

from THE SOLDIER

I

Dry leaves, soldier, dry leaves, dead leaves:
voices of leaves on the wind that bears them to destruction,
impassioned prayer, impassioned hymn of delight
of the gladly doomed to die. Stridor of beasts,
stridor of men, praisers of lust and battle,
numberless as waves, the waves singing
to the wind that beats them down.

         Under Osiris,
him of the Egyptian priests, Osymandyas the King,
eastward into Asia we passed, swarmed over Bactria,
three thousand years before Christ.

         The history of war
is the history of mankind.
        So many dead:
look at them there in the dark, look at them going,
the longest parade of all, the parade of the dead:
between then and now, seven thousand million dead:
dead on the field of battle.

        The people which is not ready
to guard its gods, and its household gods, with the sword,
who knows but it will find itself with nothing
save honor to defend—?
        Consider, soldier,
whatever name you go by, doughboy, dogface,
(*solidus,* a piece of silver, the soldier's pay,)

marine or tommy, Gods mercenary—consider our lot
in the days of the single combat. You have seen on the sea-
    shore,
in the offshore wind blown backward, a wavecrest
windwhipped and quivering, borne helpless and briefly
to fall underfoot of an oncoming seawall, foam-smothered,
sea-trapped, lost; and the roar, and the foamslide regathered,
once more to recede, wind-thwarted again: thus deathward
the battle lines whelmed and divided. The darkling battalions
locked arms in chaos, the bravest, the heroes,
kept in the forefront; and this line once broken,
our army was done for.

✿   ✿   ✿

II

In the new city of marble and bright stone,
the city named for a captain: in the capital:
under the solemn echoing dome, in the still tomb,
lies an unknown soldier.

(Concord: Valley Forge: the Wilderness: Antietam:
Gettysburg: Shiloh)

                    In the brown city,
old and shabby, by the muddy Thames, in the gaunt avenue
where Romans blessed with Latin the oyster and the primrose,
the stone shaft speaks of another. Those who pass
bare their heads in the rain, pausing to listen.

(Hastings: Blenheim: Waterloo: Trafalgar: Balaklava:
Gallipoli)

Across grey water, red poppies on cliffs and chalk,
hidden under the arch, in the city of light,

[160]

the city beloved of Abelard, rests a third,
nameless as those, but the fluttering flame
substituting for a name.

Three unknown soldiers:
three, let us say, out of many. On the proud arch
names shine like stars, the names of battles and victories;
but never the name of man, you, the unknown.
Down there runs the river, under dark walls of rock,
parapets of rock, stone steps that green to the water.
There they fished up in the twilight another unknown,
the one they call *L'Inconnue de la Seine:* drowned hands,
drowned hair, drowned eyes: masked like marble she listens
to the drip-drop secret of silence; and the pale eyelids
enclose and disclose what they know, the illusion
found like fire under Lethe. Devotion here sainted,
the love here deathless. The strong purpose turns
from the daggered lamplight, from the little light to the lesser,
from stone to stone stepping, from the next-to-the-last
heartbeat and footstep even to the sacred, to the last.
Love: devotion: sacrifice: death: can we call her unknown
who was not unknown to herself? whose love lives still
as if death itself were alive and divine?

And you, the soldier:
you who are dead: is it not so with you?
Love: devotion: sacrifice: death: can we call you unknown,
you who knew what you did? The soldier is crystal:
crystal of man: clear heart, clear duty, clear purpose.
No soldier can be unknown. Only he is unknown
who is unknown to himself.

CONRAD AIKEN

[161]

IN DISTRUST OF MERITS

STRENGTHENED to live, strengthened to die for
  medals and positioned victories?
They're fighting, fighting, fighting the blind
  man who thinks he sees,—
who cannot see that the enslaver is
enslaved; the hater, harmed. O shining O
      firm star, O tumultuous
        ocean lashed till small things go
      as they will, the mountainous
        wave makes us who look, know

depth. Lost at sea before they fought! O
  star of David, star of Bethlehem,
O black imperial lion
  of the Lord—emblem
of a risen world—be joined at last, be
joined. There is hate's crown beneath which all is
      death; there's love's without which none
        is king; the blessed deeds bless
      the halo. As contagion
        of sickness makes sickness,

contagion of trust can make trust. They're
  fighting in deserts and caves, one by
one, in battalions and squadrons;
  they're fighting that I
may yet recover from the disease, *my
self;* some have it lightly, some will die. "Man's
      wolf to man?" And we devour
        ourselves? The enemy could not

have made a greater breach in our
defenses. One pilot-

ing a blind man can escape him, but
   Job disheartened by false comfort knew,
that nothing is so defeating
   as a blind man who
can see. O alive who are dead, who are
proud not to see, O small dust of the earth
      that walks so arrogantly,
         trust begets power and faith is
      an affectionate thing. We
      vow, we make this promise

to the fighting—it's a promise—"We'll
   never hate black, white, red, yellow, Jew,
Gentile, Untouchable." We are
   not competent to
make our vows. With set jaw they are fighting,
fighting, fighting,—some we love whom we know,
      some we love but know not—that
         hearts may feel and not be numb.
      It cures me; or am I what
      I can't believe in? Some

in snow, some on crags, some in quicksands,
   little by little, much by much, they
are fighting fighting fighting that where
   there was death there may
be life. "When a man is prey to anger,
he is moved by outside things; when he holds
      his ground in patience patience
         patience, that is action or

beauty," the soldier's defense
   and hardest armor for

the fight. The World's an orphans' home. Shall
   we never have peace without sorrow?
without pleas of the dying for
   help that won't come? O
quiet form upon the dust, I cannot
look and yet I must. If these great patient
      dyings—all these agonies
         and woundbearings and blood shed—
      can teach us how to live, these
         dyings were not wasted.

Hate-hardened heart, O heart of iron,
   iron is iron till it is rust.
There never was a war that was
   not inward; I must
fight till I have conquered in myself what
causes war, but I would not believe it.
      I inwardly did nothing.
         O Iscariotlike crime!
      Beauty is everlasting
         And dust is for a time.

MARIANNE MOORE

[164]

STILL FALLS THE RAIN

The Raids, 1940: Night and Dawn

STILL falls the Rain—
Dark as the world of man, black as our loss—
Blind as the nineteen hundred and forty nails upon the Cross

Still falls the Rain
With a sound like the pulse of the heart that is changed to the
    hammer beat
In the Potter's Field, and the sound of the impious feet

On the Tomb:
               Still falls the Rain
In the Field of Blood where the small hopes breed and the
    human brain
Nurtures its greed, that worm with the brow of Cain.

Still falls the Rain
At the feet of the Starved Man hung upon the Cross,
Christ that each day, each night, nails there, have mercy on
    us—
On Dives and on Lazarus:
Under the Rain the sore and the gold are as one.

Still falls the Rain—
Still falls the Blood from the Starved Man's wounded Side:
He bears in His Heart all wounds,—those of the light that
    died,
The last faint spark

In the self-murdered heart, the wounds of the sad uncompre-
    hending dark,
The wounds of the baited bear,—
The blind and weeping bear whom the keepers beat
On his helpless flesh . . . the tears of the hunted hare.

Still falls the Rain—
Then—"O Ile leape up to my God! Who pulles me doune?—
See, see where Christ's blood streames in the firmament."
It flows from the Brow we nailed upon the tree
Deep to the dying, to the thirsting heart
That holds the fires of the world,—dark-smirched with pain
At Caesar's laurel crown.

Then sounds the voice of One who, like the heart of man,
Was once a child who among beasts has lain—
"Still do I love, still shed my innocent light, my Blood, for
    thee."

                                                EDITH SITWELL

LENINGRAD: 1943

from THE PULKOVO MERIDIAN

                                        . . . from day to day
    The calcium in our cells grows less and less
    And we grow weaker. Take me, now. Some way,
    I scratched my finger in my carelessness.
    That's three months back, as near as I can tell,
    And yet, devil take it, it will not get well.

        [166]

How painfully—still worse, how swiftly—can
Faces grow old these days! The features stand
Out, cut to birdlike sharpness by the hand,
It seems, of some ill-omened make-up man.
A pinch of ashes and a little lead—
And faces look like faces of the dead.

The teeth are bared, the mouth drawn tight, the face
Is waxen and the beard like a cadaver's
(A beard the razor hardly can displace).
The walk, without a balance center, wavers.
The pulse beneath the ashen-colored skin
Is weak. The albumin is gone. The end sets in.

Among the women many have a swelling.
They shiver constantly (though not from frost).
Their bosoms shrink to nothingness, compelling
The once-white kerchiefs to be tighter crossed.
Who would believe that once at such a breast
A child had ever sucked himself to rest?

Like melted candles in their apathy.
All the dry summaries and indications
Are here of what by learned designations
Doctors call "alimental dystrophy."
Non-Latinists, non-philologues will name
It simply hunger, but it means the same.

And after that the end is very near.
The body, rolled up in a dust-gray cover
Fastened with safety pins, and wound all over
With rope, upon a child's sled will appear,

[167]

So neatly laid out that it's plain to see
It's not the first one in the family.

VERA INBER

*Translated by Dorothea Prall Radin
and Alexander Kaun*

MANIFESTO OF THE SOLDIER
WHO WENT BACK TO WAR

KNOW this.
Spent bullets die in the mouths of the forgotten dead.
I have seen it. I have also seen buried guns, sown by the rain,
grow and blossom in the black smoke, and larks make their
        nests
between bayonet-branches.

Know this.
I have gathered thoughts and secrets twelve inches
beneath empty skulls
where stagnant water still etches the sky of day that is gone.

Know this.
I have heard the orchestra of breasts that burst like warships,
I have hoisted the sail of eyelids white with agony,
and have wet my hands in the bitter waters of heavenly seas
peopled by archangel captains.

Know this.
I know what the cold is like of those clenched hands
that seek a tombstone in the quarry of dawn
and a cross in the flight of a random swallow.

[168]

I know what it is to clutch memory
and bite it to the bursting lips:
to call out my own name
in the silence of comrades who can not answer me
or recognize me . . .

  Know this.
I have heard the lips of mortal wounds
say *Mother* . . . , *Dearest* . . . , *My son* . . . ,
in the ironclad calm of night,
and I could go on drinking in my heart
the water of untroubled quiet.

  Know this.
I have eaten the earth where I lay
as though it were food made of the world's first honey.
And I have counted the days—and the nights of heedless
    moon—
on the calendar of my scars.

  Know this.
I know what the sound is like
of a bullet which strikes the body of a comrade already dead,
and what the wind says when it strikes the harp of barbed
    wire . . .
  Know this, Comrades, and forget it.
Forget it. Forget it. Forget it.

  I will return with them.
I will return with life,—without it, even.
  The spirits that dwell in the wind will carry me,
or the young air of the accordions:
sobs and curses will carry me,

[169]

corners and avenues compel me . . .
   But never ask me. It is a secret, Comrades.
   A secret!
   Know this.

ANGEL MIGUEL QUEREMEL
Translated by Donald Devenish Walsh

ONE MORNING THE WORLD WOKE UP

ONE morning the world woke up and there was no news;
No gun was shelling the great ear drum of the air,
No Christian flesh spurted beneath the subtle screws,
No moaning came from the many agony-faced Jews,
Only the trees in a gauze of wind trembled and were fair.

No trucks climbed into the groove of an endless road,
No tanks were swaying drunken with death at the hilltop,
No bombs were planting their bushes of mud and blood,
And the aimless tides of unfortunates no longer flowed:
A break in the action at last . . . all had come to a stop.

Those trees danced, in their delicate selves half furled
And a new time on the glittering atmosphere was seen;
The lightning stuttering on the closed eyelid of the world
Was gone, and an age of horizons had dawned, soft, pearled;
The world woke up to a scene like spring's first green.

Birds chirped in waterfalls of little sounds for hours,
Rainbows, in miniature nuggets, were stored in the dews,
The sky was one vast moonstone of the tenderest blues,

[170]

And the meadows lay carpeted in three heights of flowers:
One morning the world woke up and there was no news.

OSCAR WILLIAMS

DIRGE

For the Barrel-Organ of the New Barbarism

THOSE stopped by the barrage
Came back at twelve o'clock
Haggard and mad with rage
      Came back at twelve o'clock
      The women bent with their bearing
      The men with the damned look
The women bent with their bearing;
And crying for their lost toys
Their children with eyes staring
      And crying for their lost toys
      Uncomprehending they saw
      Their ill-defended skies
Uncomprehending they saw
The machine-gun at the intersection
And in ashes the grocery store
      The machine-gun at the intersection
      Soldiers talked in subdued voices
      And a colonel looked in the other direction
Soldiers talked in subdued voices
Counting the dead counting the lame
All from the familiar places
      Counted the dead counted the lame

[171]

Their sweethearts: what will be their words?
'O my love, O my shame'
Their sweethearts: what will be their words?
They will sleep with their photos
Leaving the sky to the birds
 They will lie down with their photos
 On the stretchers of coarse linen
 Until they are buried in rows
On the stretchers of coarse linen
They are carrying away the young men
With red bellies and grey skin
 They are carrying away the young men
 But who knows what good it will do
 They will die Sergeant count ten
And who knows what good it will do
Whether they get to Saint-Omer
What will it prove between him and you
 If they get to Saint-Omer
 They'll find the enemy very close
 His armor cutting them off from *la mer*
They'll find the enemy very close
They say Abbeville has been captured
May our sins be forgiven us
 They say Abbeville has been captured
 Thus spoke the firers of shells
 Watching the columns uncaptured
Thus spoke the firers of shells
Looking like painted madness
Eyes here thoughts somewhere else
 Looking like painted madness
 A civilian passing them by
 Laughed savagely at their sadness

[172]

A civilian passing them by
Was as black as the black coal mines
Was black (if you like) as life
        He was as black as the coal mines
        That giant on his way back
        To Mericourt or to Sallaumines
That giant on his way back
Yelled at them: So what? We're through!
Whether it's thunder or flak
        Yelled at them: So what? We're through!
        Better to crack up at home
        From a slug in the belly, or two,
Better to crack up at home
Than to walk in a foreign country
Better be sealed in one's loam
        Than to walk in a foreign country
        But we're coming, we're coming back throug]
        Hearts heavy, and bellies empty
We're coming, we're coming back through
Without tears, without hope, without arms
We wanted to leave, but no
        Without tears, without hope, without arms
        Those in their peace over there
        Gave the police the alarm
Those in their peace over there
Sent us back under the bombs
Told us You cannot stay there
        Sent us back under the bombs
        So we come in all of our ranks
        No need to dig us our tombs
We come in all of our ranks
With our children, yes and our dames

[173]

No need to give us your thanks.
　　　　With their children, yes and their dames
　　　　St. Christophers of the Land
　　　　They passed by the places in flames
St. Christophers of the Land
Giants whose profiles loomed high
With not even a stick in their hand
　　　　Giants whose profiles loomed high
　　　　Thrown by anger against a white sky

Louis Aragon
Translated by S. R.

AGAIN

On the establishment of a Fascist Dictatorship in Austria February 1934

Again we smelled for days on end
The smell of powder from afar.
Again we felt for days on end
The coming war.

Again instead of prayers and tears
Shot after rifle-shot.
Again the widowed women wring
Bare hands to God.

Again the waiting and patience again—
And a little more hope to be free,
Again we hear the summons to fight
From the gallows-tree.

[174]

Again we hear the tortured cry
Merge with the burying bell,
Again it is hunger and slavery—
And our enemy, he who keeps still!

FRANTIŠEK HALAS
Translated by Karl W. Deutsch

LAOCOON

THE first shot was fired to Wagnerian music; drums bore it
    skyward . . . seaward . . .
Under the water and the blown weed. Violence in the last
    house on the last street!
The Neanderthal man at the window, the Cro-Magnon at the
    separate door!

Violence has no meaning: it is noise or motion; it is pure stress.
The duty of the civilian: not to be deafened by detonations;
To plant a forest of silence, to preserve trees of thought for the
    soldier's return . . .

(Violence like a python swallows the mind in combat.
"What do you think of?" asked the foreign correspondent.
"I think of killing Germans," said the girl sniper.)

. . . . . . to welcome the casualties with wisdom; to define the
    enemy;
To hear the grass growing under caissons, to see exiles crossing
    the bright frontiers;
To light in the mind the violent statue, to unwind the Laocoon.

DON GORDON

[175]

GRENADA

WE RODE at a trot,
We sped into battle,
The song "Little Apple"
Held in our teeth.
Ah, this little song
Hovers to this day
Over the young grass,
The steppe's malachite.
But a different song,
Of a faraway land,
My buddy carried
Along on his saddle.
He sang, while glancing
At his native fields:
"Grenada, Grenada,
Grenada of mine!"

This little song
He has learned by heart.
How came Spain's melancholy
To this Ukrainian?
Answer, Alexandrovsk,
And Kharkov, reply:
Since when have you begun
In Spanish to sing?
Tell me, O Ukraine:
Does not 'mid your corn
Lie the shaggy cap
Of Taras Shevchenko?
Wherefrom, my buddy,

[176]

Comes your song:
"Grenada, Grenada,
Grenada of mine!"

He is slow in answer,
The dreamy Ukrainian:
"Little brother, Grenada
I found in a book.
A pretty name,
A high honor.
In Spain there is
A Grenada county.
I left my hut,
I went to war,
The Grenada land
For to give the peasants.
Farewell, my dear ones,
Farewell, my kinsmen.
Grenada, Grenada,
Grenada of mine!"

On we sped, dreaming
Of mastering quickly
The grammar of battle,
The battery language.
The sun now rose,
Now set again,
My horse grew tired
Galloping the steppes.
The squadron played
The song "Little Apple"
With bows of suffering
On violins of time.

[177]

But where, O my buddy,
Is that song of yours:
"Grenada, Grenada,
Grenada of mine!"

His pierced body
Slid down to the earth.
For the first time my comrade
Has left the saddle.
I beheld: over the corpse
The moon bent down,
The dead lips breathed: "Grena . . ."
Yes! To a faraway land,
To a reach beyond the clouds,
Has gone my buddy,
And taken his song.
Since then his native fields
Have no longer heard:
"Grenada, Grenada,
Grenada of mine!"

The squadron failed to note
The loss of one warrior,
And the song "Little Apple"
They sang to the end.
Only 'cross the sky softly
Crept, after a bit,
A tearlet of rain.
New songs
Life invents.
Let us not, buddies,
Mourn for songs.

[178]

Let us not, let us not,
Let us not, my friends . . .
Grenada, Grenada,
Grenada of mine!

MIKHAIL ARKADYEVICH SVETLOV
Translated by Alexander Kaun

ALMERÍA

A DISH for the bishop, a crushed and bitter dish,
A dish of scrap iron, of ashes, of tears,
An imbedded dish, with sighs and fallen walls,
A dish for the bishop, a dish of blood from Almería.

A dish for the banker, a dish with the cheeks
Of children from the happy South, a dish
With detonations, with mad waters and ruins and dread,
A dish with broken axles and trampled heads,
A black dish, a dish of blood from Almería.

Every morning, every turbid morning of your life
You shall have it steaming and piping hot on your table:
You will push it a little aside with your soft hands
So as not to see it, so as not to digest it so many times:
You will push it a little aside between the bread and the
        grapes,
This dish of silent blood
Which will be there every morning, every
Morning.

[179]

A dish for the colonel and the colonel's wife,
At a feast in the garrison, at every feast,
Over the swearing and the spitting, with the vinous light of
   dawn
So that you may see it trembling and cold over the world.

Pablo Neruda
Translated by Angel Flores

THE INTERNATIONAL BRIGADE
ARRIVES AT MADRID

The morning of a cold month,
Of an agonizing month, soiled by mud and by smoke,
A month without knees, a sad month of siege and misfortune,
When across the wet windowpanes of my house the African
   jackals were heard
Howling with their rifles and their teeth full of blood,
Then,
When for hope we had only a dream of gunpowder, when we
   thought
That the world was full only of devouring monsters and furies,
Then, breaking through the frost of Madrid's cold month, in
   the mist
Of the dawn,
I saw with these eyes that I have, with this heart that sees,
I saw the arrival of the staunch ones, the towering soldiers
Of the thin and hard and ripe and ardent brigade of stone.

It was the grievous time when the women
Bore absence like a terrible live coal,

And Spanish death, more acid and sharp than other deaths,
Hovered over fields honored till then by wheat.

Along the streets the broken blood of men mixed
With water gushing from the shattered heart of houses;
The bones of torn children, the heartrending
Silence in mourning of the mothers, the eyes
Of the defenceless closed forever,
Were like the sadness and the lost, were like a garden spat on,
Were the faith and the flower murdered forever.

Comrades,
Then,
I saw you,
And my eyes are even now filled with pride
Because I saw you across the misty morning coming to the
        pure forehead of Castile,
Silent and firm,
Like bells before dawn,
Full of solemnity and with blue eyes coming from far away,
From your corners from your lost lost countries, from your
        dreams
Full of burnt sweetness and guns
To defend the Spanish city in which cornered liberty
Might fall and die bitten by the beasts.

Brothers, from now on
May your purity and your strength, your solemn history,
Be known to child and man, to woman and old man,
May it reach all beings devoid of hope, descend the mines cor-
        roded by sulphuric air,
Ascend the inhuman stairs of the slave,

[181]

That all the stars, that all the ears of grain of Castile and of
the world
May write your name and your bitter struggle
And your victory powerful and earthly like a red elm.
Because with your sacrifice you have caused to be reborn
The lost faith, the absent soul, confidence in the earth,
And through your abundance, through your nobility, through
your dead,
As through a valley of hard rocks of blood
Flows an immense river with doves of steel and hope.

PABLO NERUDA
Translated by Angel Flores

THE BATTLE OF THE JARAMA

BETWEEN the earth and the drowned platinum
Of olive groves and dead Spaniards,
Jarama, hard dagger, you have resisted
   The wave of the cruel ones.

From Madrid came men
With hearts gilded by gunpowder,
Like bread of ash and resistance,
   They arrived.

Jarama, you lay between iron and smoke
Like a branch of fallen crystal,
Like a long line of medals
   For the victors.

[182]

Neither caves of burning substance,
Nor choleric explosive flights,
Nor artilleries of turbid darkness
   Dominated your waters.

Your waters were drunk by those thirsty
For blood, water they drank face upward
Spanish water and olive fields
   Filled them with forgetfulness.

And ever it comes the rabid mist of sleeplessness
For a second of water and time the stream
Of the blood of Moors and traitors
Shimmered in your light like fishes
   In a bitter pool.

The rough flour of your people
Bristled with metal and bones,
Formidable and wheat-bearing like the noble
   Land they defended.

Jarama, to talk about your regions
Of splendor and dominion, my tongue is not
Adequate, and my hand is pale:
   Your dead remain there.

Your grievous sky remains there,
Your peace like stone, your starry stream,
And the eternal eyes of your people
   Keep vigil on your shores.

                              PABLO NERUDA
                              Translated by Angel Flores

[183]

BROTHER FIRE

When our brother Fire was having his dog's day
Jumping the London streets with millions of tin cans
Clanking at his tail, we heard some shadow say
'Give the dog a bone'—and so we gave him ours;
Night after night we watched him slaver and crunch away
The beams of human life, the tops of topless towers.

Which gluttony of his for us was Lenten fare
Who mother-naked, suckled with sparks, were chill
Though dandled on a grill of sizzling air
Striped like a convict—black, yellow and red;
Thus we were weaned to knowledge of the Will
That wills the natural world but wills us dead.

O delicate walker, babbler, dialectician Fire,
O enemy and image of ourselves,
Did we not on those mornings after the All Clear
When you were looting shops in elemental joy.
And singing as you swarmed up city block and spire,
Echo your thought in ours? 'Destroy! Destroy!'

Louis MacNeice

"FAR FROM THE HEART OF CULTURE"

Far from the heart of culture he was used:
Abandoned by his general and his lice,
Under a padded quilt he closed his eyes
And vanished. He will not be introduced

When this campaign is tidied into books:
No vital knowledge perished in his skull;
His jokes were stale; like wartime, he was dull;
His name is lost forever like his looks.

He neither knew nor chose the Good, but taught us,
And added meaning like a comma, when
He turned to dust in China that our daughters

Be fit to love the earth, and not again
Disgraced before the dogs; that, where are waters,
Mountains and houses, may be also men.

W. H. AUDEN

ULTIMA RATIO REGUM

THE guns spell money's ultimate reason
In letters of lead on the spring hillside.
But the boy lying dead under the olive trees
Was too young and too silly
To have been notable to their important eye.
He was a better target for a kiss.

When he lived, tall factory hooters never summoned him.
Nor did restaurant plate-glass doors revolve to wave him in.
His name never appeared in the papers.
The world maintained its traditional wall
Round the dead with their gold sunk deep as a well,
Whilst his life, intangible as a Stock Exchange rumour, drifted
        outside.

[185]

O too lightly he threw down his cap
One day when the breeze threw petals from the trees.
The unflowering wall sprouted with guns,
Machine-gun anger quickly scythed the grasses;
Flags and leaves fell from hands and branches;
The tweed cap rotted in the nettles.

Consider his life which was valueless
In terms of employment, hotel ledgers, news files.
Consider. One bullet in ten thousand kills a man.
Ask. Was so much expenditure justified
On the death of one so young and so silly
Lying under the olive trees, O world, O death?

STEPHEN SPENDER

THE KNOWN SOLDIER

THE balancing spaces are not disturbed
By the yes or no of these cantering brutes.
Frequently another robe is placed
On the unriddling skeleton of man's labor
To destroy his God-enchanted animal;
Then the hordes of murder howl
On the solemn islands of death.
But these unsorrowing angels
Still hover above my city,
And they pick golden fruit
On the orchard slopes of our destiny.

[186]

We cannot wish to hear confessions
That teach innocence; we are not possessed
Of mercy enough to pardon those whom evil
Has not fattened, whose use has not kissed guns.
What is this crazy croon of nobleness,
Of ancient human wisdom and honor?
What majesty itches on the grinning tongues
Of these who have died
That men might not live?

KENNETH PATCHEN

NOSTALGIA

My soul stands at the window of my room,
  And I ten thousand miles away;
My days are filled with Ocean's sound of doom,
  Salt and cloud and the bitter spray.
Let the wind blow, for many a man shall die.

My selfish youth, my books with gilded edge,
  Knowledge and all gaze down the street;
The potted plants upon the window ledge
  Gaze down with selfish lives and sweet.
Let the wind blow, for many a man shall die.

My soul is now her day, my day her night,
  So I lie down, and so I rise;
The sun burns close, the star is losing height,
  The clock is hunted down the skies.
Let the wind blow, for many a man shall die.

[187]

Truly a pin can make the memory bleed,
  A world explode the inward mind
And turn the skulls and flowers never freed
  Into the air, no longer blind.
Let the wind blow, for many a man shall die.

Laughter and grief join hands. Always the heart
  Clumps in the breast with heavy stride;
The face grows lined and wrinkled like a chart,
  The eyes bloodshot with tears and tide.
Let the wind blow, for many a man shall die.
March 19, 1942, Indian Ocean

KARL JAY SHAPIRO

TROOP TRAIN

IT STOPS the town we come through. Workers raise
Their oily arms in good salute and grin.
Kids scream as at a circus. Business men
Glance hopefully and go their measured way.
And women standing at their dumbstruck door
More slowly wave and seem to warn us back,
As if a tear blinding the course of war
Might once dissolve our iron in their sweet wish.

Fruit of the world, O clustered on ourselves
We hang as from a cornucopia
In total friendliness, with faces bunched
To spray the streets with catcalls and with leers.
A bottle smashes on the moving ties

And eyes fixed on a lady smiling pink
Stretch like a rubber-band and snap and sting
The mouth that wants the drink-of-water kiss.

And on through crummy continents and days,
Deliberate, grimy, slightly drunk, we crawl,
The good-bad boys of circumstance and chance,
Whose bucket-helmets bang the empty wall
Where twist the murdered bodies of our packs
Next to the guns that only seem themselves.
And distance like a strap adjusted shrinks,
Tightens across the shoulder and holds firm.

Here is a deck of cards; out of this hand
Dealer, deal me my luck, a pair of bulls,
The right to draw to a flush, the one-eyed jack.
Diamonds and hearts are red but spades are black,
And spades are spades and clubs are clovers—black.
But deal me winners, souvenirs of peace.
This stands to reason and arithmetic,
Luck also travels and not all come back.

Trains lead to ships and ships to death or trains
And trains to death or trucks, and trucks to death,
Or trucks lead to the march, the march to death,
Or that survival which is all our hope;
And death leads back to trucks and trains and ships,
But life leads to the march, O flag! at last
The place of life found after trains and death
—Nightfall of nations brilliant after war.
Australia, 1943

KARL JAY SHAPIRO

ELEGY FOR A DEAD SOLDIER

I

A WHITE sheet on the tail-gate of a truck
Becomes an altar; two small candlesticks
Sputter at each side of the crucifix
Laid round with flowers brighter than the blood,
Red as the red of our apocalypse,
Hibiscus that a marching man will pluck
To stick into his rifle or his hat,
And great blue morning-glories pale as lips
That shall no longer taste or kiss or swear.
The wind begins a low magnificat,
The chaplain chats, the palmtrees swirl their hair,
The columns come together through the mud.

II

We too are ashes as we watch and hear
The psalm, the sorrow, and the simple praise
Of one whose promised thoughts of other days
Were such as ours, but now wholly destroyed,
The service record of his youth wiped out,
His dream dispersed by shot, must disappear.
What can we feel but wonder at a loss
That seems to point at nothing but the doubt
Which flirts our sense of luck into the ditch?
Reader of Paul who prays beside this fosse,
Shall we believe our eyes or legends rich
With glory and rebirth beyond the void?

[190]

For this comrade is dead, dead in the war,
A young man out of millions yet to live,
One cut away from all that war can give,
Freedom of self and peace to wander free.
Who mourns in all this sober multitude
Who did not feel the bite of it before
The bullet found its aim? This worthy flesh,
This boy laid in a coffin and reviewed—
Who has not wrapped himself in this same flag,
Heard the light fall of dirt, his wound still fresh,
Felt his eyes closed, and heard the distant brag
Of the last volley of humanity?

IV

By chance I saw him die, stretched on the ground
A tattooed arm lifted to take the blood
Of someone else sealed in a tin. I stood
During the last delirium that stays
The intelligence a tiny moment more,
And then the strangulation, the last sound.
The end was sudden, like a foolish play,
A stupid fool slamming a foolish door,
The absurd catastrophe, half-prearranged,
And all the decisive things still left to say.
So we disbanded, angrier and unchanged,
Sick with the utter silence of dispraise.

V

We ask for no statistics of the killed,
For nothing political impinges on
This single casualty, or all those gone.

Missing or healing, sinking or dispersed,
Hundreds of thousands counted, millions lost.
More than an accident and less than willed
Is every fall, and this one like the rest.
However others calculate the cost,
To us the final aggregate is *one,*
One with a name, one transferred to the blest;
And though another stoops and takes the gun,
We cannot add the second to the first.

VI

I would not speak for him who could not speak
Unless my fear were true: he was not wronged,
He knew to which decision he belonged
But let it choose itself. Ripe in instinct,
Neither the victim nor the volunteer,
He followed, and the leaders could not seek
Beyond the followers. Much of this he knew;
The journey was a detour that would steer
Into the Lincoln Highway of a land
Remorselessly improved, excited, new,
And that was what he wanted. He had planned
To earn and drive. He and the world had winked.

VII

No history deceived him, for he knew
Little of times and armies not his own;
He never felt that peace was but a loan,
Had never questioned the idea of gain.
Beyond the headlines once or twice he saw
The gathering of a power by the few
But could not tell their names; he cast his vote,
Distrusting all the elected but not the law.

[192]

He laughed at socialism; *on mourrait*
Pour les industriels? He shed his coat
And not for brotherhood, but for his pay.
To him the red flag marked the sewer main.

VIII

Above all else he loathed the homily,
The slogan and the ad. He paid his bill
But not for Congressmen at Bunker Hill.
Ideals were few and those there were not made
For conversation. He belonged to church
But never spoke of God. The Christmas tree,
The Easter egg, baptism, he observed,
Never denied the preacher on his perch,
And would not sign Resolved That or Whereas.
Softness he had and hours and nights reserved
For thinking, dressing, dancing to the jazz.
His laugh was real, his manners were home made.

IX

Of all men poverty pursued him least;
He was ashamed of all the down and out,
Spurned the panhandler like an uneasy doubt,
And saw the unemployed as a vague mass
Incapable of hunger or revolt.
He hated other races, south or east,
And shoved them to the margin of his mind.
He could recall the justice of the Colt,
Take interest in a gang-war like a game.
His ancestry was somewhere far behind
And left him only his peculiar name.
Doors opened, and he recognized no class.

[193]

His children would have known a heritage,
Just or unjust, the richest in the world,
The quantum of all art and science curled
In the horn of plenty, bursting from the horn,
A people bathed in honey, Paris come,
Vienna transferred with the highest wage,
A World's Fair spread to Phoenix, Jacksonville,
Earth's capitol, the new Byzantium,
Kingdom of man—who knows? Hollow or firm,
No man can ever prophesy until
Out of our death some undiscovered germ,
Whole toleration or pure peace is born.

XI

The time to mourn is short that best becomes
The military dead. We lift and fold the flag,
Lay bare the coffin with its written tag,
And march away. Behind, four others wait
To lift the box, the heaviest of loads.
The anesthetic afternoon benumbs,
Sickens our senses, forces back our talk.
We know that others on tomorrow's roads
Will fall, ourselves perhaps, the man beside,
Over the world the threatened, all who walk:
And could we mark the grave of him who died
We would write this beneath his name and date:

Epitaph

Underneath this wooden cross there lies
A Christian killed in battle. You who read,
Remember that this stranger died in pain;

[194]

And passing here, if you can lift your eyes
Upon a peace kept by a human creed,
Know that one soldier has not died in vain.
New Guinea, 1944

KARL JAY SHAPIRO

ABEL

MY BROTHER Cain, the wounded, liked to sit
Brushing my shoulder, by the staring water
Of life, or death, in cinemas half-lit
By scenes of peace that always turned to slaughter.

He liked to talk to me. His eager voice
Whispered the puzzle of his bleeding thirst,
Or prayed me not to make my final choice,
Unless we had a chat about it first.

And then he chose the final pain for me.
I do not blame his nature: he's my brother;
Nor what you call the times: our love was free,
Would be the same at any time; but rather

The ageless ambiguity of things
Which makes our life mean death, our love be hate.
My blood that streams across the bedroom sings:
'I am my brother opening the gate!'

DEMETRIOS CAPETANAKIS

ONCE as we were sitting by
The falling sun, the thickening air,
The chaplain came against the sky
And quietly took a vacant chair.

And under the tabacco smoke:
"Freedom," he said, and "Good" and "Duty."
We stared as though a savage spoke.
The scene took on a singular beauty.

And we made no reply to that
Obscure, remote communication,
But only stared at where the flat
Meadow dissolved in vegetation.

And thought: O sick, insatiable
And constant lust; O death, our future;
O revolution in the whole
Of human use of man and nature!

ROY FULLER

A WRY SMILE

THE mess is all asleep, my candle burns.
I hear the rain sharp on the iron roof
And dully on the broad leaves by the window.
Already someone moans, another turns
And, clear and startling cries 'Tell me the truth!'

The candle throws my shadow on the wall
And gilds my books: to-night I'd like to bring
The poets from their safe and paper beds,
Show them my comrades and the silver pall
Over the airfield, ask them what they'd sing.

Not one of them has had to bear such shame,
Been tortured so constantly by government,
Has had to draw his life out when the age
Made happiness a revolution, fame
Exile, and death the whimsy of a sergeant.

But without envy I remember them,
And without pity look at my condition:
I give myself a wry smile in the mirror
—The poets get a quizzical ahem.
They reflect time, I am the very ticking:

No longer divided—the unhappy echo
Of a great fault in civilization; inadequate,
Perhaps, and sad, but strictly conscious no one
Anywhere can move, nothing occur,
Outside my perfect knowledge or my fate.

Roy Fuller

ELEGY ON THE EVE

Not from the glory of the cloud's pile and rift
        The magnetic ray will fall
To guide me to a goal wherefrom I former fell
Through the sexual sky into a skin's shift.

[197]

Nor shall the North Star that takes sailors home
        Point me to my haven
Where I can know my heart shall not again be hove,
        And I shall harbour.

O dolphins of my delight I fed with crumbs,
Gambading through bright hoops of days,
How much me now your acrobatics amaze,
Leaping my one-time ecstasies from Doldrums!
        And you, my constants, gulls,
Hung like a wreath of love on the mast they follow,
Waft with their wings through calms the boat below,—
        My friends, my fine fellows.

What rock was hit, what mad storm I came through,
Bringing my hulk to the home of a grave through Europe,
When danger of war darkened already dark blue,
Bombed cockle love and the overloaded tramps of hope?
Life is torpedoed and like a *Titanic* goes under
        Threshing her ensigns
Against the dreadnought seas of blood and thunder
        That flood our visions.

How many ophelias float far out that Atlantic
Lost to how many parents who lie also rocking,
        Lost in Europe's sinking:
    Frilled with pathetic private fancies,
The suicidal weeds of liberal thinking
That gave them bound and gagged to the frantic sea?
        How many boys now happy on seashores shall
        Listen to the roar of war in a Nazi shell?

Be gay, be gay, John o' London, for paradise nevertheless
Lies low on the horizon not so far as the Hebrides,

But glimmers and glows a gunshot to the west
            Among the Hesperides.
Whistle now and sing like Cock Robin in a corner
Who with a gun at his breast could also sing
            With heaven round the corner.

Go down, John Doe, with a sigh and a shout of joy
            To join the Seven Sleepers
Who found the Ephesian Palace of the tomb; and
Not the gold bullet or silver bugle can awaken
To a chaos of fate that silences the jay,
            On its twigs of June
Those who sleep deep in the hole of a cipher
With a triumphant smile no gas can weaken.

So laugh at the Junker that coughs across space
Dropping its blood clots on your roof, and deride
The ridiculous bomb that lays you on your face
            With flowers and friends beside,
Giving the gift of Peace with a shot of war,
The Ephesian Palace for your ramshackle shed:
            By whom also we wear
The crown of wounds changing to stars on the head.

At night I stood on a Southern hill
When the moon accosted me like a woman who died,
        And with a word told me I was not dead
            For she saw passion in me still.
'Passion is tides of the blood I do not govern,
But moves under the self-destroying sun.
Passion is suicide by which life is proven:
        I am the dead, the only happy one.'

                              GEORGE BARKER

THE DEATH OF THE
BALL TURRET GUNNER

FROM my mother's sleep I fell into the State
And I hunched in its belly till my wet fur froze.
Six miles from earth, loosed from its dream of life,
I woke to black flak and the nightmare fighters.
When I died they washed me out of the turret with a hose.

RANDALL JARRELL

A REFUSAL TO MOURN THE DEATH,
BY FIRE, OF A CHILD IN LONDON

NEVER until the mankind making
Bird beast and flower
Fathering and all humbling darkness
Tells with silence the last light breaking
And the still hour
Is come of the sea tumbling in harness

And I must enter again the round
Zion of the water bead
And the synagogue of the ear of corn
Shall I let pray the shadow of a sound
Or sow my salt seed
In the least valley of sackcloth to mourn

The majesty and burning of the child's death.
I shall not murder

The mankind of her going with a grave truth
Nor blaspheme down the stations of the breath
With any further
Elegy of innocence and youth.

Deep with the first dead lies London's daughter,
Robed in the long friends,
The grains beyond age, the dark veins of her mother
Secret by the unmourning water
Of the riding Thames.
After the first death, there is no other.

DYLAN THOMAS

SONG

(*On seeing dead bodies floating off the Cape*)

THE first month of his absence
I was numb and sick
And where he'd left his promise
Life did not turn or kick.
The seed, the seed of love was sick.

The second month my eyes were sunk
In the darkness of despair,
And my bed was like a grave
And his ghost was lying there.
And my heart was sick with care.

The third month of his going
I thought I heard him say

[201]

'Our course deflected slightly
On the thirty-second day—'
The tempest blew his words away.

And he was lost among the waves,
His ship rolled helpless in the sea,
The fourth month of his voyage
He shouted grievously
'Beloved, do not think of me.'

The flying fish like kingfishers
Skim the sea's bewildered crests,
The whales blow steaming fountains,
The seagulls have no nests
Where my lover sways and rests.

We never thought to buy and sell
This life that blooms or withers in the leaf,
And I'll not stir, so he sleeps well,
Though cell by cell the coral reef
Builds an eternity of grief.

But Oh! the drug and dullness of my Self;
The turning seasons wither in my head;
All this slowness, all this hardness,
The nearness that is waiting in my bed,
The gradual self-effacement of the dead.

ALUN LEWIS

"HEUREUX QUI COMME ULYSSE . . ."

LUCKY like Cook to travel and return
    Or like MacArthur of the golden fleece
    Is he who drops his bluey and in peace
Lives out among his mates the rest of his time.

For me, I can't remember what we burn
    In open hearths at home that smells so sweet—
    Only recall the scent; and incomplete
I fight in foreign lands for what I earn.

No, not the Rhine, the Niger or the Thames
Sluggish with history and reflected flames
Is worth a drop of Yarra. Till time ends

Nothing of Europe holds a hope for me,
Nor is the mistral worth the wind that blends
Bluegum and cordite with the southern sea.

JOHN MANIFOLD

FIFE TUNE

(6/8) for 6 Platoon, 308th I.T.C.

ONE morning in Spring
We marched from Devizes
All shapes and all sizes
Like beads on a string,

[203]

But yet with a swing
We trod the bluemetal
And full of high fettle
We started to sing.

She ran down the stair
A twelve-year-old darling
And laughing and calling
She tossed her bright hair;
Then silent to stare
At the men flowing past her—
These were all she could master
Adoring her there.

It's seldom I'll see
A sweeter or prettier;
I doubt we'll forget her
In two years or three,
And lucky he'll be
She takes for a lover
While we are far over
The treacherous sea.

JOHN MANIFOLD

THE DRILL

I WATCH them on the drill field, the awkward and the grave,
The slow to action and the easily incensed,
The tall plowboys, the pale clerks, the fast men with a dollar,
The frightened adolescents, and those whose eyes explode
Like bombs or, like exhausted coals, lie dead.

They wheel and turn. The eternal convolutions
Of close-order drill—Right Flank or To the Rear—
Hold them as though, somnambulists, they moved
In the imposing caverns of some recurring dream
Where the only escape is to awake. But the night is very long.

The feet march on through the heavy summer morning,
The bodies are anonymous in their cotton khaki clothes,
And the faces, too, are all of a piece. Concealed at last from
  life
Are the weak chin, the nose too large, the forehead rutted and
  worn,
And the eyes too small, and the lips too fleshy or thin.

For the moment the accounts are all settled, the goods have all
  been sold,
The last delivery made, the last essay sent to the printer,
The elevator gone on its last strict voyage, the truck turned the
  last corner,
The last issue of bonds taken up, the last class attended,
The last row planted, the last payment made on the house.

The platoon moves past me on the field of summer
And disappears into the darkness of our time,
A body of men, none known, none recognized,
Crossing my road for a little space. They go
Into the sun and the summer and the waiting war.

Seen for an instant and gone. Yet I felt between us
A bond not of country but of faith and love,
And I thought of an old phrase: "Whither thou goest,
I will go." And it seemed that the summer morning
Spoke out in a voice like song, that the air was full of singing.

[205]

And something said, "They come and they go away,
The patient and the small. They go away into the sun,
Their names are forgotten and their few works also,
But when they go they take their weapons with them,
And they leave behind them houses heavy with honor."

And I thought: *It is enough.* As I stood in a field
In Virginia in deep summer, while all around me
The trees dipped and the grass rustled, I heard the sound
Of platoons of men marching toward the crouching future,
And the voices of our approaching generations.

HARRY BROWN

ON THE EVE OF THE FEAST
OF THE IMMACULATE CONCEPTION: 1942

MOTHER of God, whose burly love
Turns swords to plowshares, come, improve
    On the big wars
And make this holiday with Mars
Your Feast Day, while Bellona's bluff
Courage or call it what you please
    Plays blindman's buff
    Through virtue's knees.

Freedom and Eisenhower have won
Significant laurels where the Hun
    And Roman kneel
To lick the dust from Mars' bootheel
Like foppish bloodhounds; yet you sleep

Out our distemper's evil day
                And hear no sheep
                Or hangdog bay!

Bring me tonight no axe to grind
On wheels of the Utopian mind:
                Six thousand years
Cain's blood has drummed into my ears,
Shall I wring plums from Plato's bush
When Burma's and Bizerte's dead
                Must puff and push
                Blood into bread?

Oh, if soldiers mind you well
They shall find you are their belle
                And belly too;
Christ's bread and beauty came by you,
Celestial Hoyden, when our Lord
Gave up the weary Ghost and died,
                You shook a sword
                From his torn side.

Over the seas and far away
They feast the fair and bloody day
                When mankind's Mother,
Jesus' Mother, like another
Nimrod danced on Satan's head.
The old Snake lopes to his shelled hole;
                Man eats the Dead
                From pole to pole.

                                ROBERT LOWELL

[207]

THE BOMBER

BOMBER climb out on the roof
Where your goggled pilots mock,
With positive disproof,
David's and Sibyl's bluff.
"Will God put back the clock
Or conjure an Angel Host
When the Freedoms police the world?"
O Bomber your wings are furled
And your choked engines coast.
The Master has had enough
Of your trial flights and your cops
And robbers and blindman's buff,
And Heaven's purring stops
When Christ gives up the Ghost.

The air is gassy and dry,
Bomber climbing the crest
Of the daredevil sky;
For this is the clinker day
When the burnt out bearings rest,
And we give up the Ghost.
At dawn like Phaeton
To the demolishing sun
You hurtled the hollow boast
Until you lost your way.
Now you dive for the global crust.
How can frail wings and clay
Beat down the biting dust
When Christ gives up the Ghost?

Bomber like a god
You nosed about the clouds
And warred on the wormy sod;
And your thunderbolts fast as light
Blitzed a wake of shrouds.
O godly Bomber, and most
A god when cascading tons
Baptized the infidel Huns
For the Holy Ghost,
Did you know the name of flight
When you blasted the bloody sweat
And made the noonday night:
When God and Satan met
And Christ gave up the Ghost?

ROBERT LOWELL

"THIS LONELINESS FOR YOU IS LIKE THE WOUND"

THIS loneliness for you is like the wound
That keeps the soldier patient in his bed,
Smiling to soothe the general on his round
Of visits to the somehow not yet dead;
Who, after he has pinned a cross above
The bullet-bearing heart, when told that this
Is one who held the hill, bends down to give
Folly a diffident embarrassed kiss.
But once that medalled moment passes, O,
Disaster, charging on the fever chart,

Wins the last battle, takes the heights, and he
Succumbs before his reinforcements start.
Yet, now, when death is not a metaphor,
Who dares to say that love is like the war?

DUNSTAN THOMPSON

"I BURN FOR ENGLAND
WITH A LIVING FLAME"

(Written just before the author's death)

I BURN for England with a living flame
In the uncandled darkness of the night.
I share with her the fault, who share her name,
And to her light I add my lesser light.
She has my arm—who had my father's arm,
Who shall not have my unborn children's arm.

I burn for England, even as she burns
In living flame, that when her peace is come
Flame shall destroy whoever seeks to turn
Her sacrifice to profit—and the homes
Of those who fought—to wreckage,
In a war for freedom—who were never free.

GERVASE STEWART

[210]

"THE LANDSCAPE LIES
WITHIN MY HEAD"

THE landscape lies within my head,
The floating mast, the shattered hull,
The sodden fingers of the dead
Climb up the rock which is my skull.

The chequered flag, the ribboned tires,
The flaming wreckage flung behind,
The suicides, the theatre fires,
Work out their progress in my mind.

The silver note slim on the bow
Explores the detail of my brain,
Mates with the idealistic flow
And falls in semitones again.

Brain canvas, colours, love and hate,
Slick brush my eyeballs, thought my guide,
And three for sixpence while you wait
I paint the slums, the countryside.

GERVASE STEWART

THE THRUSH

(To N. A. W.)

I PLUCKED a throstle from the throat of God;
Into her teeming freckled breast I sent
Wanton destruction.

[211]

Boldly she sat upon the bough,
Outright she sung her song of joy
Constant and careless.

Sadist upon that holy spot,
I raised my gun—and shot.

Plucking immortal chords from life,
I stopped her song and stole
Her immortality.
Profiled she was against the sky,
A taste of world's reality
Amongst chaos, man's strategy.

Lord, much loved you her full-throated song.
Lord, pray forgive me—I did wrong.
                              TIMOTHY CORSELLIS

NOTES ON THE POETS AND THE POEMS

NOTES ON THE POETS AND THE POEMS

AESCHYLUS—the founder of Greek Tragedy wrote in all some ninety plays, of which seven are extant, but the elegiac couplet he composed for his tomb in Gela, Sicily, makes no mention of them. "Beneath this stone," the veteran of Marathon and Salamis wrote, "lies Aeschylus, Euphorion's son, who perished in wheat-bearing Gela; of his prowess the grove of Marathon can speak, or the long-haired Persian who knows it well."—S. R.

AIKEN, CONRAD—was born in Georgia and was graduated from Harvard in 1912; he lived for years in England—before World War II at Rye, since the war at Brewster, Massachusetts. *The Soldier* is the latest of a series of long poems which began to appear in 1914. All of his work is marked by musical values.—R. E.

ALBIZZI, NICCOLO DEGLI—Little is known of the poet who wrote this 'prolonged sonnet,' other than that he came of a famous Arezzo family prominent in Guelph party politics, and that he wrote in the school of the 'dolce stil nuovo' that preceded Dante. Dante Gabriel Rossetti, himself the son of an Italian and a notable Victorian poet and painter, included this translation in his *The Early Italian Poets* (1861), admitting his inability to discover any other work by its author or the circumstances which gave rise to it.—S. R.

ALCAEUS—a contemporary of Sappho and member of a noble family of Mitylene, served as a soldier in the war against the Athenians (606 B.C.). Like the Roman poet Horace six centuries later, who also appropriated his invention, the Alcaic metre, Alcaeus is reputed to have fled from battle with the loss of his shield. Of his hymns, drinking-songs and poems assailing tyranny, only fragments survive.—S. R.

AMON-RE—the divine Lord of Thebes, was credited by the priests who inscribed this Hymn celebrating Egypt's greatest Pharaoh on a black granite tablet of the main sanctuary at Karnak, with its authorship. The translation was abridged from Breasted's *Ancient Records of Egypt* by Tom Prideaux and Josephine Mayer in their *Never to Die: The Egyptians in their own words* (1938). A slightly later poem of the Early Empire quoted in that volume, "The Hard Lot of the Soldier," records Thutmose III's seventeen Syrian campaigns from the G.I. point of view: "How his masters are many . . . They go in and out of their offices in the Palace. They say 'Produce the man that can work.' . . . his body is worn out, he is dead while yet alive. He receiveth his corn ration when released from duty, but it is uneatable . . . He is called up . . . His body is broken with dysentery . . . In the village are his wife and children, but he dieth and doth not reach it."—S. R.

ANONYMOUS—"In most lighter verse," writes Louis MacNeice in his *Modern Poetry,* "the 'grain of salt' and the 'urge to nonsense' are blended. For example, the magnificent Irish ballad 'Johnny, I hardly knew ye' is on the surface of it just a normally light-hearted ballad on the subject of war, but why this ballad has such peculiar appeal is, I think, partly because it contains a sardonic criticism of war typical of the hardened cynicism which familiarity with war breeds in ordinary people."

APOLLINAIRE, GUILLAUME—He was killed in the last year of World War I. His original name was Wilhelm de Kostrowitzki. A child in the time of Baudelaire and Rimbaud, he was too young to attend Mallarmé's Tuesday gatherings in the Rue de Rome for the expounding of Symbolism. He was twenty at the turn of the century and personified the new ideas of Cubism, which he introduced into poetry with *Alcools* in 1911. He was out to destroy Symbolism.—R. E.

ARAGON, LOUIS—first came into prominence as one of the founders and leaders of the Surrealist school of art and writing; he was one of its first priests in the field of letters, immediately following his participation in World War I. Following his Surrealistic productions, for a brief period he wrote poetry in a rather more orthodox vein. He then became an active Communist. He was on the editorial staff of *Ce Soir*, a Communist evening paper which was suppressed a week before the beginning of World War II. In this war he was a prisoner, was evacuated from Dunkirk, and has a *croix de guerre* with palm, and the *medaille militaire*. His novels are characterized by simplicity and the use of every-day language. Throughout the occupation of France, Aragon aided the resistance movement and wrote freely, if feverishly, in verse; some of the poems of this new burst of work were translated and commented upon in this country by Malcolm Cowley.—R. E.

ARISTOPHANES—College boys read his plays, but men have not practised, no, nor women either! the principles set forth in his "Lysistrata." *Contra bellum est contra natura!* But his purpose was to ridicule, and perhaps only incidentally to change institutions.—R. E.

AUDEN, W. H.—It was my experience to secure for Auden his first job in the United States as a guest member of the English department at St. Mark's School, Southborough, Massachusetts. I remarked publicly at the time that Auden's coming to America was as significant a literary event as Eliot's going to Europe was in the expatriotic days. Auden attempted psychologically to overthrow the upper middle class society from which he stemmed by coming to this country. He has since become a citizen. His attempts to penetrate the mysteries of religion do not seem to some to comport with his witty and apparently non-religious personality. He taught at Swarthmore and in 1945 went to Germany to instruct. The sonnet included in this volume was written following a visit to the China war front in 1938.—R. E.

BARKER, GEORGE—was educated in London at the L.C.C. School, Chelsea. He published his first volume of poems in 1933. After the incumbency of William Empson, he went to Japan as a teacher in the Imperial University at Tokyo. He did not stay long and returned via the United States, as Empson had done. He read his poems at Harvard and stayed for a while in New York with Oscar Williams. He is now in England. Faber and Faber, who published his *Poems, Calamiterror,* and *Lament and Triumph,* have just brought out a new book of his work.—R. E.

BASHŌ, MATSURA—a lyric poet of the 17th century, with a great reputation in Japan as a moralist, contributed a variation to the immemorial, attenuated staple of Japanese poetry, the *hokku,* a five-line stanza with the first and third lines containing five syllables and the other three seven; Bashō appears to have heightened the impressionism of this Liliputian vehicle by dropping some of the syllables.— S. R.

'BHAGAVAD-GITA'—was the name given to the third, latest historically, and most famous part of the Mahabharata, the national poem of India. The dialogue which constitutes the *Bhagavad-gita* grows out of Arjuna's compunction at the idea of fighting his way to a kingdom and Sri Krishna's answer (the passage we quote). In the succeeding verses the duties of caste above all other obligations are exalted, but their practise is shown to be compatible with the self-mortification of the Yoga philosophy as well as with the deepest devotion to the Supreme Being. Another notable English rendition from the Sanskrit was done recently by W. B. Yeats and Shree Purohit Swami.—S. R.

BLAKE, WILLIAM—His life was a seventy-years war: a war against intolerance, poverty, cruelty, fear, derivative art; a war for truth, kindness, the regeneration of man, artistic integrity. Equally great as mystic, artist and lyric poet he was neglected during an incredibly productive lifetime and was buried in an unmarked grave in Bunhill Fields.—S. R.

BLOK, ALEKSANDR—was born in St. Petersburg (Leningrad). His father was professor of mathematics at Warsaw. In 1903 he married Mendeleyev's daughter,

[216]

and the following year his first book of poems was published. His most famous poems—"The Scythians," with its prophetic message of pacts and wars to come, and "The Twelve," a vivid symbolic paean to the October Revolution—dramatize the conflict in Blok of disillusionment and national idealism.—S. R.

BOKER, GEORGE HENRY—Romantic leanings showed up in his first blank verse tragedy, *Calaynos* (1849). He wrote many plays in his native Philadelphia. His greatest achievement was *Francesca da Rimini* (1855), a verse tragedy of high literary quality as well as good theater, telling of the love of Paolo and Francesca and their murder by Prince Lanciotto, his brother and her husband. The play was successfully revived (1885-6). Boker served as Minister to Turkey (1871-5) and Minister to Russia (1875-9). *Nydia* and *Sonnets: A Sequence on Prcfane Love* were published in 1929.—R. E.

BORN, BERTRANS DE—He was intimately connected with Richard Coeur de Lion, and exercised a powerful influence over the destinies of the royal family of England.—R. E.

BROWN, HARRY—From Maine, he went for a short while to Harvard. He edited the lively *Vice Versa* with Dunstan Thompson. His light verse was published copiously by *The New Yorker*. He was one of the founders of *Yank*, and wrote the successful short novel *A Walk in the Sun*. He invented Artie Greengroin. New Directions published his more serious verse in *The Violent*.—R. E.

'BRUNANBURH'—This ballad, inserted in the "Anglo-Saxon Chronicle," and buried there till Tennyson made his superb rendition of it into English, celebrated Æthelstan's defeat of Anlaf of Ireland and Constantine of Scotland in 937 A.D. —S. R.

BYRON, GEORGE GORDON, LORD—wrote the stirring stanzas on the Duke of Brunswick's ball following a visit to the field of Waterloo in May 1816; they were incorporated in Canto III of *Childe Harold's Pilgrimage*, published in November of the same year. Byron had left England in April, never to return. On the Continent he was already regarded as the apostle of liberty, but it was not till seven years later that his ideas approached the test of action. In 1823, "called to the colors" by the Greek revolutionaries, he bought a ship and sailed from Leghorn to Missolonghi. His presence served to unite the embattled insurgents; he prepared to capture the fortress of Epacto; he was offered the governor-generalship of the enfranchised areas; but the climate and his earlier excesses denied him the apotheosis of battle; he died in April of 1824, aged thirty-six, the hope of his last poem unrealized: "Seek out, less often sought than found, A soldier's grave, for thee the best; Then look around and choose thy ground, And take thy rest."—S. R.

CAEDMON—the earliest English Christian poet, is supposed to have lived some time between the years 658 and 731. The Venerable Bede, whose theological history is source for what little we know of his life and for the only poem that can be certainly ascribed to his name, a nine-line 'Hymn,' tells us that Caedmon was discovered uttering "verses he had never heard," was taken to the Abbess Hild at Streanaeshalch where he became an inmate, and there versified the Scriptures. The lines quoted in this book are from "Genesis," one of the three so-called "Caedmon Poems" discovered in a manuscript of 1000 A.D.—S. R.

CALLINUS—was an early Greek elegiac poet, of uncertain date, who lived in Ephesus perhaps in the 7th Century B.C. Only a few fragments of his work have been preserved. He is the first poet known to have written in elegiacs.—R. E.

CAMPBELL, THOMAS—son of a Glasgow merchant, was educated at Glasgow University. He is remembered mainly for his splendid war songs; in addition to "Hohenlinden," he also wrote such war songs as "The Battle of the Baltic," "Ye Mariners of England" and "The Soldier's Dream."—R. E.

CAPETANAKIS, DEMETRIOS—left Greece for England in 1939. When he died there of fever in 1944, aged thirty-two, he had learned to write, as by a miracle, English poetry of the first order. Edith Sitwell has written of "Abel": "The voice that

[217]

speaks to Abel is sometimes the voice of mankind speaking to the individual who must die that his brother may live—is sometimes the voice of democracy, the brotherhood that may fail us through sheer incomprehension . . . Compared with this intensely strange poem, with its great profundity, leading us to the centre of the earth, the core of the heart, the central impulse from which thoughts and movements spring, many poems written by the stricken young of our time seem but surface poems." Beginning as a disciple of Stefan George, Capetanakis was said to have been "cured" by Gray, Donne and Blake; wanting always to *be* loved, he rejected Rilke to whom love's essence was the act of loving.—S. R.

CHU YUAN—is placed by Lin Yutang among the three or four greatest poets of China, and among the most difficult. Arthur Waley, describing his famous "Falling into Trouble," a love-allegory of the relations between the poet and his king, remarks: "In this poem sex and politics are curiously interwoven, as we need not doubt they were in Chu Yuan's own mind." As happens so often in art, the style which prodigiously expressed the abnormal psychology of the master, in his followers led to excessive mannerism.—S. R.

CLOUGH, ARTHUR HUGH—was educated at Rugby and Balliol College, Oxford. He became a Fellow of Oriel, but later principal of University Hall, London. Then he became an examiner in the Education Office. After his death at Florence, Matthew Arnold wrote "Thyrsis" commemoratively. The lyric included in this book shows the marks of spiritual agitation caused by the religious doubts rampant in his time. It was differently construed when Winston Churchill quoted it in a famous speech at a critical moment of the world's history.—R. E.

CORSELLIS, TIMOTHY—was a Second Officer in the British Air Transport Auxiliary, killed in action at the age of 21.—R. E.

COWPER, WILLIAM—was the son of a rector of Great Birkhamstead, was educated at Westminster School, and called to the bar in 1754. He suffered from fits of depression and tried to commit suicide in 1763. He lived in retirement with Morley Unwin at Huntington in 1765 as a boarder in his house and after Unwin's death removed with Mary, Unwin's widow, to Olney, where the 'Olney Hymns' were published in 1779. He became engaged to Mrs. Unwin, but had another attack of mania in 1773. In 1782 were published eight satires written at the suggestion of Mrs. Unwin. In 1782 he wrote *John Gilpin* and in 1784 *The Task*. In 1786 he moved, with Mrs. Unwin, to Weston where he wrote short poems, published posthumously, such as *Yardley Oak, On the Loss of the Royal George* and *To Mary*. In 1785 he undertook to translate Homer; he turned out so many lines per day, the translation appearing in 1791. Mrs. Unwin died in 1796. After four years of gloom over her loss, he died. His poetry breaks away from the classical style of Pope and heralds the naturalism of Wordsworth.—R. E.

CRANE, STEPHEN—in 1892 borrowed $700 to print *Maggie: A Girl of the Streets*. The copies were piled in a New York storeroom, unsold, unread. The following year, twenty-three, and with no war experience whatsoever, he wrote what is generally considered the first realistic account of warfare, and one of the two or three greatest of all war-novels, *The Red Badge of Courage*. Beyond the fact that William Dean Howells is supposed to have read him some of Emily Dickinson's then unpublished poems at lunch one day, there is no clue to the startling originality of *Black Riders and Other Poems* (1895). The following year Crane shipped with filibusters for Cuba. In 1897 he covered the Turkish War as a correspondent in Greece. In 1898 he was cited for bravery while covering the Spanish-American War. *War Is Kind* was written in England in 1899. Two years later, Crane died, aged thirty, at Badenweiler, Black Forest.—S. R.

CUMMINGS, E. E.—served in the Ambulance Corps in World War I, following his graduation from Harvard. Through a censor's error he spent three months in a detention camp, a circumstance which led to the composition of *The Enormous Room* and to attitudes regarding war, society and bureaucracy which found their biting, lyrical expression in *Tulips and Chimneys* (1924) and the succession of poems that have followed, without truce, to the present.—S. R.

DICKINSON, EMILY—The niceties of her oddities are still studied, and not even the psychiatrists know quite what to make of her reclusive, peculiar, and potent soul. We can still speculate on the changes in her poetry had she gone, say, to Paris. She feared Europe.—R. E.

DONNE, JOHN—in 1596, when he was twenty-three, engaged himself for foreign service under the Earl of Essex, and "waited upon his lordship" on board the "Repulse" in the great naval victory of June 11th. During this, and his subsequent voyage to the Azores in 1597, he wrote several of the highly-charged metaphysical poems which led his contemporary Ben Jonson to remark (setting the tone for three centuries of myopia): "He wrote all his best pieces ere he was twenty-five."—S. R.

EHRENBURG, ILYA—was born in Kiev of a wealthy Jewish family, spending his childhood in Czarist Moscow which he later described as "stale with the odor of hot, sour beer." He was tutored there by a professional hypnotist. At 13 he visited Berlin alone. In 1905 he helped build barricades in the Presnya district and organized strikes. In 1909 he was imprisoned for eight months as an agitator. In 1914 his travels found him living in France where he was rejected at first by the French army as "unfit for service" and served as a stevedore loading explosives. Hearing of the growing fame of his poems in Russia, the Paris police promptly reversed their decision, sending him to the front with the admonishment "You'll write differently there." As the poet put it, "I did. I shed my mysticism entirely." With the outbreak of the October Revolution, Ehrenburg returned to Russia, narrowly escaping the White Guard pogrom in Kiev, becoming shortly one of the USSR's most famous novelists. His dispatches from the front in World War II made him a national hero—at least until 1945 when the violence of his propaganda counselling hatred of the German people was officially rebuked in *Pravda*.—S. R.

ELIOT, T. S.—was born in St. Louis, was graduated from Harvard in 1910, and studied at the Sorbonne and at Merton College, Oxford. He instructed in philosophy for one year at Harvard, then departed in 1914 for Europe, returning only in 1932 to lecture on poetry at Harvard, and in 1944 to lecture at the University of Virginia. In the interim he was a banker for a time. *The Waste Land* appeared in 1922. *Prufrock and Other Observations*, his first book of poems, had appeared in 1917 and *Poems* in 1919.

In 1923 he became editor of "The Criterion," which flourished for many years as the leading journal of serious literary opinion in English. He became a British subject in 1927.

The Sacred Wood, 1920, *For Lancelot Andrewes*, 1928, and *After Strange Gods*, 1934, are three of his prose works.

Ash Wednesday appeared in 1930, a poem directly opposed to *The Waste Land*, one of the finest religious and lyrical poems of the century.

The Rock, 1934, was less actively theatrical than *Murder in the Cathedral*, 1935, which achieved popularity on both sides of the Atlantic. *The Family Reunion*, which followed it, was less popular, perhaps more densely psychological, as a play. *Old Possum's Book of Practical Cats*, 1939, showed his light-verse aptitude.

Four Quartets, 1943, Eliot's latest poetical work, is composed of four poems printed at first separately: "Burnt Norton," "East Coker," "The Dry Salvages," and "Little Gidding."—R. E.

EMERSON, RALPH WALDO—The first article of his faith was the primacy of mind: mind is supreme, eternal, absolute, one, manifold, subtle, living, immanent in all things, flowing, permanent, self-manifesting. The universe is the result of mind, with nature its symbol. His second article connects individual intellect with the primal mind, from which it can draw wisdom.—R. E.

ENNIUS—There is very little known about him. His full name was Quintus Enaclus. We have only fragments of his work left, but it is fairly certain that he introduced the hexameter into Latin verse. Not only did he introduce it, but some of his isolated lines are as good as any Latin hexameters ever written. Even the few fragments we have show that he was an enthusiastic and gifted experimenter. In fact, he would try anything, going at times to ridiculous lengths. His spirit was far more free and less bound by tradition and custom than was usual among the Romans. That may be attributable to the fact that he came from southern Italy—Apulia—and may have had Greek blood in him. At any rate, the story goes that he said he had three hearts because he spoke three languages—Greek, Latin, and Oscan. If the story is true it shows that he had an uncommon realization of the importance of language. His principal work was a history of Rome in verse, of which the selection included in this book is a fragment. The editors are indebted for the above information to John Wight.—R. E.

EURIPIDES—began his military service in 466 B.C. with garrison service on the Athenian frontier, an experience he doubtless drew upon fifty years later when the cynical Athenian aggression against Melos stirred him, as it did his great contemporary Thucydides, to his greatest work. Then it was that the aged, rebellious dramatist saw fit to picture Greece's proudest legendary triumph, the capture of Troy, as seen in all its barbarity through the eyes of "The Trojan Women." —S. R.

FROST, ROBERT—His latest book "A Masque of Reason" shows an excellent independence of mind. His wit is caustic, but not malicious: he merely tries to bait the truth in its lair.—R. E.

FULLER, ROY—The Hogarth Press printed *A Lost Season* in 1944, his second book of poems. Roy Fuller was born at Oldham, Lancashire, in 1912. He is married and has one child. He was conscripted to the British Navy in April, 1941, and transferred to the Fleet Air Arm half a year later. *The Middle of a War* was published in 1942.—R. E.

GEORGE, STEFAN—was associated with Baudelaire and Mallarmé in Paris and with the Pre-Raphaelite group in London, being in Germany the leader of the "art for art's sake" school of poetry. He gathered about him a group of disciples; by the time of his death he had become a legend. Articles appeared discussing what was discussed at his salon, but his works were never widely read in America. He has a similarity with Nietzsche in that he believed in certain ideas which may be said to have formed a body of doctrine which nurtured the ideas behind Fascism. —R. E.

GORDON, DON—He is a contributor to Harpers and other magazines, and has recently appeared in anthologies. He lives in California, publishing his first book of poems in 1943.—R. E.

GRENFELL, JULIAN HENRY—was the son of William Henry Grenfell, afterwards first baron Desborough. He was educated at Eton and Balliol College, Oxford. He obtained a commission in the army in 1910 and was killed early in the Great War. No other poem of his equals "Into Battle" and many of his poems were in the nature of light verse.—R. E.

GUMILEV, NICOLAI—reacted from the Symbolists and, rejecting the metaphysical style of Ivanov, became a champion of restraint and clarity, moving toward the Latin and the classical. He founded the Petersburg Guild of Poets and gave lessons in his ideas to young poets. His poetry is masculine and bracing, full of the romance of adventure and fighting, and of the exotic charm of tropic lands.—R. E.

HALAS, FRANTIŠEK—Mr. F. C. Weiskopf, author of the "Hundred Towers," "The Firing Squad," etc., in 1937 won a Czechoslovak State Prize for translating the poems of Halas into German, including the poem translated for this book by Dr. Karl W. Deutsch.—R. E.

[220]

HARDY, THOMAS—who considered his impressive and popular novels "pot-boilers" and who, from his fifty-seventh year till his death thirty years later wrote nothing but poetry, has still to be properly assessed as poet. The anthologists have given him lip service, grudgingly. His war-poems alone, of which the selection in this book are but a sampling, are unexcelled.—S. R.

HOMER—There is doubt as to both his dates and birthplace. His very existence has been questioned. And periodically the theory has been advanced that he was a woman; this theory was argued most recently in the days of Samuel Butler. Eratosthenes made him almost contemporary with the events he relates, the 12th c. B.C. Herodotus, partially confirmed by Thucydides, placed him in the 9th c. Some modern critics date him as late as the 7th c. His language shows him familiar with the Ionic and Aeolic dialects of the coast of Asia Minor; Chios and Smyrna have both claimed him.

The *Iliad* and the *Odyssey* were compositions intended to be chanted or recited. Nobody knows who wrote them down. The Age of Alexander was a time of much study of the poems, notably by Zenodotus, Aristophanes, and Aristarchus. Our present text derives from a vulgate text as early as Plato, if not earlier. It is based mainly on two manuscripts of the 10th and 11th centuries now in Venice.

Aristotle mentions the unity of plot and perfection of structure in Homer, and is impressed by the vividness of expression throughout the writing. Matthew Arnold gives rapidity, plainness in thought and diction, and nobility as the chief Homeric characteristics. Homer's works came to be regarded in ancient times as a source of wisdom and were generally and constantly quoted. After World War I T. E. Lawrence translated the *Odyssey*, as had Pope before him.—R. E.

HOPKINS, GERARD MANLEY—Phare, Father Lahey, Pick and others have all of them, and more recent critics, not said the last word. Neither did he say it to Canon Dixon or Coventry Patmore. His unalterable originality can be seen as much in his notes about clouds as in any line of his fragments.—R. E.

HORACE—would have retired to a farm, say in Brittany, or in Pennsylvania, and contemplated, in these times, the nature of man. He would have made no more of it than he did when he lived, and would have celebrated wine, women, and song, with a certain aloofness and disinterest.—R. E.

HOUSMAN, A. E.—His comments on war, like his comments on life, and on the Latin poets Juvenal, Manilius and Lucan to whose editing he brought a lifetime of erudition, were brilliantly mordant. Man was "a stranger and afraid in a world I never made" and the poet could give his soul stoic comfort only with the thought that life was "but for a season: Let us endure an hour and see injustice done." The impeccable form, derived from the Scottish Border ballads, was enough to contain this 'attitude' in almost heroic finality.—S. R.

HUGO, VICTOR—was characterized by Anatole France as "one who vibrates with such emotion he has no need to be intelligent" and André Gide when asked recently whom he considered France's greatest poet answered with the old quip "Victor Hugo—alas!" The poet himself, in one of his less egotistical moments placed himself "au centre de tout comme un echo sonore." Son of a Napoleonic general, Hugo had his first glimpses of war from the perspective of an unwelcome invader's entourage in Naples and Madrid. Beginning his career as a royalist and a classicist, he shifted to republicanism and romanticism in time to ride the crest of both latter waves. "Exiled" to the Channel Islands in 1852 where, as Harold Nicolson put it "he revelled in martyrdom for seventeen years," Hugo returned to Paris in triumph in 1870 to enjoy for his last fifteen years a celebrity and an influence probably no other poet has enjoyed in his lifetime.—S. R.

INBER, VERA—wrote "The Pulkovo Meridian," from which the stanzas we quote are taken, during the siege of Leningrad. "The poet," wrote Alexander Kaun in his *Soviet Poets and Poetry*, "muses and daydreams (of a brown crust of rye-bread) as she lies in bed gloved and booted, under two fur coats, a kerchief protecting her head. No electricity, no fuel, no food, and even the water pipes are out of order, so that the citizens make their way to the Neva River and stand in line in front of an ice hole . . . These experiences among 'luxuriating winter' do not dampen, however, the fire of loyalty to the cause . . . Vera Inber has poured into her poem the noble tragedy of a people ready to suffer and die so that the life they love may not be extinguished by mechanized brutality." Starting her career as a "constructivist," a school that sought economy of means by introducing prose methods into poetry, Vera Inber found herself in the traditional meters of stanzaic narrative.—S. R.

JARRELL, RANDALL—His second book of poems, *Little Friend, Little Friend,* is being published this year; his first, *Blood for a Stranger,* came out in 1943. The year before he enlisted in the Air Corps as a pilot. He washed out after thirty hours flying time, and is now a Sergeant C.N.T. operator, stationed at Tucson, Arizona. One of the Kenyon poets under Ransom, his work began with heavy, non-lyrical tread, but has opened up in his war subjects with a great deal of fierce and direct vision.—R. E.

KIPLING, RUDYARD—was born in Bombay, India. At the age of seventeen he became assistant editor of the *Civil and Military Gazette* in Lahore. From 1889 to 1899 he travelled in China, Japan, Africa, Australia and North America. *Barrack Room Ballads,* containing the poem in this volume and establishing his reputation as a poet, appeared in 1892. Properly·condemned as an apologist for naked imperialism, Kipling's enormous popularity suffered little, but his stature as a poet became unjustly involved; the scales were adjusted in recent years, by Eliot and Auden among others.—S. R.

LEWIS, ALUN—was teaching secondary school in one of the mining valleys of his native Wales when the war broke. His first book, *Raider's Dawn* (1941) reflected this background and his reactions to a year of service spent in England. War had already usurped the major part of his consciousness when his second book, *Ha! Ha! Among the Trumpets* appeared. Lieutenant Lewis was killed in an accident while on active service in India in May, 1944.—S. R.

LI PO—considered by many China's greatest poet, was born in Szechwan province, a descendant in the ninth generation of the Emperor Hsing-Sheng. His life is legend. We are told that he had a passion for fencing, drinking, adventure and poetry. That he saw, and understood, war is abundantly clear. Less credible is the romantic story that he drowned trying to kiss the reflection of his face by moonlight while travelling by boat on an imperial mission.—S. R.

LILIENCRON, DETLEV VON—See Preface.

LONGFELLOW, HENRY WADSWORTH—His hatred of war sprang from a true serenity of the spirit and native goodness, but the expression of that hatred, in an otherwise powerful poem, was burked by a characteristic weakness for moralizing. His first book was hailed by Poe who later called him a plagiarist. The abolitionists called his *Poems of Slavery* "perfect dishwater beside Whittier." He died the most celebrated American poet, but his poems, overpraised in his own time, as Untermeyer has said, have been underrated in ours.—S. R.

LOWELL, ROBERT—whose first book, *Land of Unlikeness* (1944), left no doubt of his stature as a poet, had already been publicly marked as a Catholic, a conscientious objector and a violator of family tradition. Son of a retired naval commander, grandson of a martial poet and anti-papist, and heir to a Boston family tradition that boasted members in every war since the Revolution, he tried to enlist twice, then became convinced the bombings of total war were unprincipled and anti-Christian. In October, 1943, Lowell was sentenced to a year and a day in Federal prison. Conrad Aiken has remarked the "angry and violent use of Catholic symbolism" in the first of Lowell's two poems in this collection. Vaughn, Crashaw and Donne are recalled but never imitated.—S. R.

MacNeice, Louis—like his friend and contemporary Stephen Spender, observed the effect of bombing on men and cities from the vantage-point of a fire-watcher during the London blitz of 1940-42. Earlier, in his *Autumn Journal,* he had depicted the atmosphere of tension and guilt that led up to the outbreak of World War II. His translation of Aeschylus' *Agamemnon* was written before the war, while he was teaching Greek at London University.—S. R.

Manifold, John—born in Melbourne and educated at Cambridge, was working as a translator with a publisher in Germany when the war broke out in 1939; he escaped to join the British Army, serving first in West Africa, later in France. He is presently a captain in the Intelligence Corps with the British occupation forces in Germany. John Day is planning to publish his *Selected Poems* in the Spring of 1946, making Manifold probably the first Australian poet to be published in this country.—S. R.

Melville, Herman—His prodigious novel *Moby Dick* was ignored for the most part until 1920; his poetry was re-discovered even later. In the 'fifties of the last century *Typee* and *Omoo* made him briefly famous; but the greater work, "broiled in hell-fire" as he put it, won him only abuse. *Battle-Pieces and Aspects of the War* (1866) were written in his decline. The poet who had written "Give me a condor's wing! Give me Vesuvius' crater for an inkstand!" spent the nineteen years of neglect and failure that followed in New York as an outdoor customs inspector.—S. R.

Milton, John—was educated at St. Paul's School and at Christ's College, Cambridge, where he took his B.A. in 1629 and his M.A. in 1632. After leaving Cambridge he lived with his father at Horton, reading steadily in the classics and preparing himself for his vocation as poet, from 1632 to 1637. *L'Allegro* and *Il Penseroso, Comus* and *Lycidas,* belong to this period. Twenty years elapsed without further poetry, excepting sonnets. In Italy (1637-1639) Milton visited Grotius and Galileo, who was in prison. Milton's ideas on episcopacy, the liberty of the press, and divorce are generally known. After he became blind, Andrew Marvell was the third, successively, of his secretaries. Milton was three times married. *Paradise Lost* dates from 1642, is said to have been finished in 1663, but the copyright agreement was not signed until 1667. *Paradise Regained* and *Samson Agonistes* were published together in 1671. He died from the gout and was buried beside his father, in St. Giles', Cripplegate, London.—R. E.

Moore, Marianne—Her unique contribution to modern poetry was first stated by T. S. Eliot in the introduction he wrote to her *Selected Poems* in 1935; before that she had been known to a smaller circle through her acting editorship of *The Dial* (1925-1929). "In Distrust of Merits," one of the six poems that make up her most recent book, *Nevertheless,* was hailed by W. H. Auden in a review in 1944 as the outstanding war poem of World War II.—S. R.

Neruda, Pablo—is in the consular service in Mexico, a native of Chile. He also has served in the consular service in Rangoon, Calcutta, and Madrid and has traveled in the Orient. Like T. S. Eliot, his work depicts the decay of society, some of it tinged with the grim and the grotesque. His is one of the best-known names in modern Latin American poetry.—R. E.

Niles, Nathaniel—Inventor, theologian, preacher, politician and man of business, was born in Rhode Island and died in Vermont. His magnificent song, recently brought to light by Richard F. Goldman in *Landmarks of Early American Music,* receives the following mention in *The Dictionary of American Biography:* ". . . His one attempt at poetry, an ode called "The American Hero," was written in celebration of the battle of Bunker Hill. Set to music it gained wide popularity during the Revolutionary War. Posterity will not regret that thereafter Niles turned his talents to other fields."—S. R.

O'Sheel, Shaemas—was born in Brooklyn, New York, as James Shields; he changed his name to the Irish equivalent as a result of activity in the Irish Independence movement while attending Columbia University. He is most widely known by

[223]

the poem included in this volume. The book from which it is taken, *Jealous of Dead Leaves* (1928) contains poems revised and selected from his two earlier books, *The Blossoming Bough* (1911) and *The Light Feet of Goats* (1915). O'Sheel is now living in New York City, is active in publicizing the work of the younger "proletarian" poets.—R. E.

OWEN, WILFRED—See Preface and Introduction.

PARKER, MARTIN—See Preface.

PATCHEN, KENNETH—*The Dark Kingdom* continued the long geographies of his religious experience which Patchen enunciated in *The Journal of Albion Moonlight*. He overthrew the security of literary form in *Before the Brave* and has struggled in a massive consciousness of evil to reproduce his sensory knowledge of it in works which are in the nature of phantasmagoria. *The Teeth of the Lion* and *The Cloth of the Tempest* are other titles.—R. E.

PEACOCK, THOMAS LOVE—met Shelley in Italy. His devotion to Shelley's posthumous reputation and to the furthering of his works has justly been hailed. He was not so swashbuckling a figure as Trelawney but shared the ideas and lives of the Romantics. Arthur Symons has written of him: "Peacock's learned wit, his satire upon the vulgarity of progress, are more continuously present in his prose than in his verse . . . They are like no other verse: they are startling, grotesque, full of hearty extravagance, at times thrilling with unexpected beauty . . . The masterpiece, perhaps, is *The War Song of Dynas Vawr*, which is, as the author says in due commendation of it, 'the quintessence of all war songs that ever were written . . . of all the tendencies and consequences of the military.' "
—R. E.

PÉGUY, CHARLES—France's great mystical poet, declared himself an atheist in 1892 at the time he was serving his three-years military training in the French Army. His conversion to Catholicism came in 1908. "Blessed are those who die . . ." was written, prophetically, in 1913. In 1914 Péguy, aged forty-one, was called up as a 2nd Lieutenant. He was killed leading a charge at Villeroy in September of that year.—S. R.

POUND, EZRA—His reaction to World War I was passive and literary; he was living in England 1917-19, serving as London Editor of the *Little Review* (Chicago). His reaction to World War II was non-literary, but active; in 1941 he began those Fascist propaganda broadcasts by short-wave from Rome for which he was subsequently indicted for treason. "These died . . . ," written at the peak of his powers in the 20's, perfectly expressed the disillusionment with the first war and its peace then widely felt.—S. R.

PROPERTIUS—was born at Assisi about 50 B.C. and became, when his first volume of elegies was published, the friend of Vergil and Ovid but not of Horace and Tibullus. Postgate reconstructs his character as foppish, sensitive, self-indulgent, voluptuous, and his style as difficult and disorderly, learned and allusive, vague and given to excessive exaggeration, but withal full of a fresh imaginative power and humor, expressed in striking, appropriate and unconventional words.—S. R.

QUEREMEL, ANGEL MIGUEL is considered one of the best poets Venezuela has produced in recent years. He spent many years in Spain as a consular official; there he partook of the atmosphere of Alberti and Lorca. He wrote ballads. Returning to Venezuela, he joined the "Viernes" group in 1936 and probably influenced some of the younger poets toward mysticism.—R. E.

RILKE, RAINER MARIA—Imperial Germany's greatest poet probably owed his hatred of war to his father, a schizophrenic officer who first dressed the child up as a girl, called him René, and gave him dolls to play with, and then at the age of ten plunged him thus equipped into the nightmare of five years in St. Poelten's military academy. Only less traumatic was his experience as a clerk in the War Department in 1914-18, when he neither wrote nor read.—S. R.

RIMBAUD, JEAN-ARTHUR—was the son of an infantry captain, received his introduction to war in the formative year of his life, 1870-1. He was sixteen, and his native Charleville had been cut off from Paris by the Prussians. He described the bourgeois 'gesticulating with the notable ferocity of non-combatants.' He predicted that the Germans would turn into 'a nation of slaves serving a military machine.' Escaping to Paris, he enlisted with the Communards, barely escaping the ferocious retribution of the White Terror but receiving the full impact of barracks' depravity. Nevertheless it has been said that but for the luck of a strenuous exposure to advanced grammar at a very early age, Rimbaud would never have mastered the language in time to become one of its most fertile users by the age of seventeen, when he gave it all up with abrupt, violent cessation.
—S. R.

ROSENBERG, ISAAC—See Preface.

SANDBURG, CARL—in one of his characteristic earlier poems, "Old Timers," has "an ancient reluctant conscript" soliloquize as follows: "On the soup-wagons of Xerxes, I was a cleaner of pans . . . Redheaded Caesar picked me for a teamster. He said 'Go to work, you Tuscan bastard . . . And I had my arm shot off at Spottsylvania Court House." The same sense of the immediacy of the past and of the pathos of history's repetitive blows upon the back of the common man may be observed in the later and more subtle war poems. Sandburg's experience with war began at the age of 20 when he enlisted in Company C, Sixth Illinois Volunteers, taking part in the Puerto Rico campaign of the Spanish American War. "Poetry," he was to write, "is the harnessing of the paradox of earth cradling life and then entombing it."—S. R.

SASSOON, SIEGFRIED—wounded and invalided home in 1917 after three years in the trenches, threw his Military Cross in the Channel and announced publicly that he would serve no more. Hoping for a courts martial, he was declared "temporarily insane" and shipped to Palestine where he fought two more years, became a captain. In 1920 he toured the United States, delivering anti-war talks and reading his poems.—S. R.

SHAKESPEARE, WILLIAM—Of Shakespeare nothing need be said. He said all.—R. E.

SHAPIRO, KARL JAY—In his first, adolescent *Poems* (privately printed, 1935), he described war in a simple Marxist dichotomy, but with premonitions in the final poem: "Turn down the jet within the sacred heart; You cannot love." In "The Fly," 1941, he packed by transference, all the disgust with basic training. "Scyros" had described induction in a setting of cosmic tragicomedy. From "Nostalgia," written on the Indian Ocean in 1942, through "Troop Train" (Australia, 1943) to "Elegy for a Dead Soldier" (New Guinea, 1944) there is a steady enlargement of comprehension and sympathy from the personal to the universal. "It is not the platitudinous comparison with the peace," writes Shapiro in the preface to *V-Letter* (1944), "or the focus on the future that should occupy us; but the spiritual progress or retrogression of the man in war, the increase or decrease in his knowledge of beauty, government and religion."
—S. R.

SHIRLEY, JAMES—whose *The Cardinal* has been called "the last great Elizabethan play," stopped writing for the stage in 1642 in accordance with the Puritan edict promulgated that year. His *Contention of Ajax and Ulysses* closes with the lines quoted in this anthology, lines which used to be sung to Charles I and which are said to have terrified by their implications, Cromwell. Shirley and his wife are believed to have died of exposure in the Great Fire that devastated London in 1666.—S. R.

SIMONIDES—was one of the great masters of the elegy and epigram. He was probably the most prolific lyric poet of Greece, but in depth and newness of ideas, and in poetic force, he was inferior to Pindar. It is recorded that he was reproached by his contemporaries because he sold his poems for money, being the first one to do so.—R. E.

[225]

SITWELL, EDITH—and her two brothers, Osbert and Sacheverell, received considerable attention because of their combined poetical efforts. More actively than her brothers, Miss Sitwell studied the possibilities of verbal tricks for the enlivening of diction. She is, among other things, "strikingly different from other poets in adapting poetry to modern musical, mainly dance, rhythms; in her own words, studying 'the effect that texture has on rhythm, and the effect that varying and elaborate patterns of rhymes and of assonances and dissonances have upon rhythm.'" Her Collected Poems appeared in 1930. Her early recordings of verse were exciting, but were baroque, rococo, cacophanous, a medley of circus-like music. She was a deft entertainer. Her later work includes *Street Song*, 1942, which contains the poem included in this book, and *Green Song and Other Poems*, 1944, both of which invade more serious realms of poetry than theretofore confronted.—R. E.

SOPHOCLES—Of the three great writers of tragedy, Sophocles was central, in other ways than by date. He represents, in the last analysis, the balance of the best Greek thought. Aeschylus was in a sense amorphous, Euripides in a sense decadent. Sophocles increased the number of actors to three, a change which greatly enlarged the scope of the action. He has been imitated, as lately as by O'Neill, but never equalled. He is allowed to have brought the drama to the highest degree of perfection of which it is susceptible.—R. E.

SPENDER, STEPHEN—His "Ultima Ratio Regum" was one of a group of poems inspired by the Spanish Civil War, written following a tour of the front the poet made with a group of British writers sympathetic to the Loyalist cause. Another group of distinguished poems grew out of the London blitz of 1940-42, in which Spender took an active part as a fire-warden; these are included in his latest book, *Ruins and Visions*.—S. R.

STEVENS, WALLACE—was born in Reading, Pennsylvania, graduated from Harvard, and practiced law in New York. He now lives in Hartford, Connecticut, where he is vice-president of the Hartford Accident and Indemnity Co. His poem "The Soldier's Wound" originally appeared in *The Kenyon Review* as part of a group entitled "Esthétique du Mal."—S. R.

STEWART, GERVASE—joined the Fleet Air Arm in 1940 at the age of 20, was commissioned a Sub Lieutenant and became a pilot. He was killed in action the following year. Educated at Cambridge where he was Chairman of Debates and editor of *Granta*, the young poet composed enough to make two books of poems, *No Weed Death* and a second soon to appear.—S. R.

SVETLOV, MIKHAIL ARKADYEVICH—A civil-war piece written before the recent conflict in Spain, "Grenada" took the USSR by storm. Its author was already renowned for his descriptions of guerrilla fighting. Most of his poems, Professor Kaun tells us, are sharpened by a dichotomy of love and hatred, breathe a fierce loyalty to the revolution and the party, celebrate collective triumphs.—S. R.

THOMAS, DYLAN—His *Selected Writing*, with an introduction by J. L. Sweeney, is to be brought out this year by New Directions. Born in Wales, and presently writing film scripts for a living, Thomas has been called the first considerable surrealist poet writing in English.—S. R.

THOMPSON, DUNSTAN—He and Harry Brown were contemporaries at Harvard and edited *Vice Versa* before the war. Lowell was there also, but went to Kenyon, where was Jarrell. Thompson was born in New London, Connecticut in 1918. His first book, *Poems*, was published by Simon and Schuster in 1944. It showed a startling and remarkable facility in the use of poetic language, a subtle control of long stanzas and complicated musical patterns; while not notable for total profundity, the book was an excellent first serious approach to a career.—R. E.

TOURNEUR, CYRIL—Tourneur was a contemporary of Webster. Whether he could have written "The White Devil" is a matter of conjecture, but they both came late in the Elizabethan age and threw it to seed with massive, lavish, and sometimes monstrous growths of words. Restraint was out of control, the blank verse grew spotty with broken lines, but Tourneur's imagination had the grandeur of the lurid.—R. E.

TYRTAEUS—flourished in Sparta during the Second Mysennian War (c.650 B.C.) in which he served. It is said also that he tried to compose the internal difficulties then besetting his warlike city. His poems, elegiac, in the Ionic dialect, some of them written to stimulate the Spartan soldier to heroism in battle, survive in twelve fragments.—S. R.

VALÉRY, PAUL—His early fascination with da Vinci explains much about his reticence in publishing. He would spend years before he would put down a line, an excellent practice of austerity. The aridity of his poems is compensated for by their depth, the depth of the ether.—R. E.

VERGIL—Vergil had eyes where Homer had not, but he did not see as much. In his last moments he was anxious to burn the whole manuscript of the Aeneid, showing a mature doubt about the value of what he did see; he directed his executors either to improve it or to commit it to the flames.—R. E.

VULGARIUS, EUGENIUS—is described by his translator, Helen Waddell, as "a timid and eager scholar, devoted to Seneca, dreaming of a revival of learning that he did not live to see, an age of gold when Charlemagne would be again glorious, and Cato tell his tales and Apollo sing." It seems that he challenged, albeit mildly, Papal infallibility; Sergius IV clapped him into Monte Cassino, then had him brought to Rome, where he quoted Seneca's "The fear of death is worse than death itself," recanted, and when released wrote shrill odes praising the Pope's magnanimity. "It is not a heroic story," his translator concludes, "but once at least his very defects, the scholar's timidity and wistfulness and anger at all the waste and cruelty of things, goaded him to a fragment of great and passionate verse."—S. R.

WHITMAN, WALT—was born in Huntington, Long Island, N. Y. He was the second of nine children of Walter Whitman, a farmer, carpenter, and Quaker, and Louisa (Van Velsor) Whitman, who was of mixed Dutch and Welsh descent. The oldest and youngest of the children were imbeciles. Walt called himself that to distinguish his name from his father's. He was slow of movement, and large, and had a placid disposition, but he was also extremely sensitive and neurotic. While working on newspapers he wrote conventional verse. In 1848 he went to New Orleans with his brother Jeff for three months; this trip later grew into a legend of great duration and, on his own confidence, the production of six apocryphal children. Back in New York, he practised oratory and the then accredited phrenology. In 1855 came the first edition of Leaves of Grass, a thin book published at Whitman's expense. The next edition, of 1856, was no longer thin. During his life eleven editions, each larger than its predecessor, appeared. Whitman wanted to be hailed by the common man, who in fact never understood him, but was uneasy when instead Emerson wrote him "I greet you at the beginning of a great career." During the Civil War Whitman lived in Washington, where he stayed for eleven years; he visited Northern and Southern hospitals as a nurse, on his own, unofficially. Out of his many experiences grew his war poems. In 1873 he had a light stroke of paralysis. He lived at 328 Mickle Street, Camden, N. J. where he eventually became a permanent invalid. He characterized himself as "a child, very old."—R. E.

WILLIAMS, OSCAR—started writing poetry for the second time in 1937 after a sixteen-year silence. He has since written two books of verse, The Man Coming Toward You and That's All That Matters, and edited a series of annual anthologies. His collection of war poems from World Wars I and II appeared in the Spring of 1945 under the title The War Poets.—S. R.

WOLFE, CHARLES—was educated at Trinity College, Dublin, served as curate of Donoughmore, County Down, from 1818 to 1821. "The Burial of Sir John

[227]

Moore" is apparently based on Southey's narrative in the *Annual Register* and was first published in the *Newry Telegraph* in 1817. Wolfe wrote no other poem of comparable distinction. His *Remains* were published in 1829.—R. E.

WOLKER, JIRI—grew up in the Czech manufacturing town of Prostějov. He attended the Gymnasium, and later the University of Prague, but died of tuberculosis at the age of 24. Dr. Karl W. Deutsch supplies the following information. Wolker did all his creative writing between the ages of 16 and 24. His first published work was the beautiful and sensitive *Diary of the Boy Scout Jiří Wolker*. Despite his youth, the deep influence of his poetry on the youth of Czechoslovakia, particularly among young workers and students, is "unequalled in the history of Czech letters." His lyrical poems and ballads have been reprinted again and again, and there is a comprehensive edition of his works in two volumes. Critics have seen Wolker's peculiar quality in his combination of gentle and very sensitive lyrics with a militant sympathy for the poor and suffering, and with his militant faith in the struggle for their liberation. Wolker thus became the poet of the labor movement, whose most militant party he supported, but his verses appealed at the same time to the entire people wherever it found itself confronted with social or national oppression. Wolker has been called the most Czech, and at the same time, the most internationalistic of the young lyricists. During the Nazi occupation of Czechoslovakia, the verses of the dead boy-poet were reprinted abroad, and copies of these new editions accompanied the soldiers of the Czech legions on their fighting march to their homeland.—R. E.

WORDSWORTH, WILLIAM—He owed a great deal to sister Dorothy, but nobody would have believed in the nineteenth century that he had had an illegitimate child in France. In his youth he was for the French Revolution, yet retired to the Lakes to contemplate a stone.—R. E.

YEATS, W. B.—the greatest of the Irish poets, and by many considered the most considerable poet of this century writing in English, was born at Sandymount, near Dublin, the son of a well-known painter. He saw no service in World War I, remained aloof from the conflict, the poem in this volume being one of the few in which he expressed explicit protest. His later poem "The Second Coming"—with its lines "The best lack all conviction, while the worst are filled with passionate intensity"—envisioned World War II with apocalyptic imagery.—S. R.

ACKNOWLEDGMENTS

ACKNOWLEDGMENTS

For permission to reprint the copyrighted poems in this volume, acknowledgment is made to the following poets, literary agents and publishers:

Conrad Aiken and New Directions
for two passages from *The Soldier* (Poets of the Year, 1944)

C. Bell & Sons, Ltd. (London)
for the passage from B. B. Rogers' translation of the *Lysistrata* of Aristophanes

Basil Blackwell
for "Salamis" from G. M. Cookson's *Four Plays of Æschylus*

Brandt & Brandt
for three selections from E. E. Cummings' *Collected Poems*, published by Harcourt, Brace & Company. Copyright, 1923, 1931, 1935, 1938 by E. E. Cummings
for "The Dug-Out" by Siegfried Sassoon from *Picture Show*. Copyright, 1920, by E. P. Dutton

Chapman and Hall (London)
for eight passages from *The Song of Roland,* translated by Charles Scott-Moncrieff

Chatto & Windus (London)
for "Strange Meeting," "Greater Love," and "The Show" by Wilfred Owen
for "Break of Day in the Trenches," and "Returning, We Hear the Larks" by Isaac Rosenberg

Clarendon Press (Oxford)
for the translations by T. F. Higham, Professor E. R. Dodds, Gilbert Highet and George Allen, in *The Oxford Book of Greek Verse in Translation,* edited by T. F. Higham and C. M. Bowra

Columbia University Press
for "The Song of the Valkyries" from Hollander, *Old Norse Poems*

Creative Age Press
for "One Morning the World Woke Up" from *That's All That Matters* by Oscar Williams

Caresse Crosby
for the three translations from the French by Selden Rodman, published in Vol. I, Number 1 of *Portfolio*

Babette Deutsch and Avrahm Yarmolinsky
for the translation of "The Scythians" by Aleksandr Blok

Duell, Sloan & Pearce, Inc.
for "Dirge" etc. by Louis Aragon from *Le Crève Coeur*

Don Gordon and "The Quarterly Review of Literature "
for "Laocoon" by Don Gordon

Harcourt, Brace & Company, Inc.
for "A.E.F." from *Smoke and Steel* by Carl Sandburg. Copyright, 1920, by Harcourt Brace & Co.
for selection from *The Agamemnon of Aeschylus* translated by Louis MacNeice

Little, Brown & Company
  for "My Triumph Lasted Till the Drums" and "Success Is Counted
    Sweetest" from *The Poems of Emily Dickinson* edited by Martha
    Dickinson Bianchi and Alfred Leete Hampson
Liveright Publishing Corporation
  for "Lament of the Frontier Guard" and for the passage from "Hom-
    age to Sextus Propertius," from *Personae* by Ezra Pound
  for "They Went Forth to Battle but They Always Fell" from *Jealous
    of Dead Leaves* by Shaemas O'Sheel
Robert Lowell and The Cummington Press
  for "The Bomber" and "On the Eve of the Feast of the Immaculate
    Conception: 1942"
C. F. MacIntyre
  for the translations from Detlev von Liliencron, Rainer Maria Rilke,
    Paul Valéry and Anonymous
The Macmillan Company
  for "Elegy on the Eve" from *Selected Poems* by George Barker
  for "Channel Firing" and "The Man He Killed" from *Collected Poems*
    and selections from *The Dynasts* by Thomas Hardy
  for "In Distrust of Merits" from *Nevertheless* by Marianne Moore
  for "An Irish Airman Foresees His Death" from *Collected Poems* by
    William Butler Yeats
Klaus Mann
  for E. B. Ashton's translation of Stefan George from *The Heart of
    Europe* published by L. B. Fischer
New Directions
  for "The Drill" from *The Violent* by Harry Brown
  for translations of Pablo Neruda by Angel Flores
  for translations of Angel Miguel Queremel by Donald Devenish
    Walsh from *An Anthology of Contemporary Latin American Poetry*
    edited by Dudley Fitts
The New Republic and Oscar Williams
  for "A Refusal to Mourn the Death, by Fire, of a Child in London,"
    by Dylan Thomas
Oxford University Press, New York
  for "The Soldier" from *Poems* by Gerard Manley Hopkins
Partisan Review
  for "Death of the Ball-Turret Gunner" by Randall Jarrell
Penguin New Writing (London)
  for "Elegy on the Eve," by George Barker, published in *Penguin
    New Writing* No. 18, July-September 1943
  for "Song" by Alun Lewis published in No. 17, April-June 1943
Random House, Inc.
  for "Ultima Ratio Regum" from *Ruins and Visions* by Stephen Spender.
    Copyright, 1942 by Stephen Spender
  for "Far from the Heart of Culture" by W. H. Auden
  for "Brother Fire" from *Springboard* by Louis MacNeice

[233]

Reynal and Hitchcock, Inc.
for "Troop Train," "Nostalgia," and "Elegy for a Dead Soldier" from *Person, Place and Thing* and *V-Letter and Other Poems* by Karl Shapiro

The Marcel Rodd Company
for selections from *Bhagavad-Gita, The Song of God,* translated by Swami Prabhavananda and Christopher Isherwood. Published by The Marcel Rodd Company, Hollywood. *192 pages $2.00*

George Routledge and Sons, Ltd. (London)
for "The Thrush" by Timothy Corsellis
for "Heureux Qui Comme Ulysse . . ." and "Fife Tune (6/8) for 6 Platoon, 308th I.T.C." by John Manifold from *More Poems from the Forces,* edited by Keidrych Rhys, 1943

Simon and Schuster, Inc.
for "This Loneliness for You Is Like the Wound" from *Poems,* 1944, by Dunstan Thompson

Edith Sitwell and Anne Watkins, Inc.
for "Still Falls the Rain" from *Street Song,* 1942, by Edith Sitwell

Wallace Stevens and The Kenyon Review
for "The Soldier's Wound" from *Esthétique du Mal* by Wallace Stevens

University of California Press
for "Grenada" by M. Svetlov and "Leningrad" by Vera Inber from *Soviet Poets and Poetry* edited by Alexander Kaun and Dorothea Prall Radin

University of Chicago Press
for "Hymn of Victory: Thutmose III" from *Ancient Records of Egypt,* Volume II, by James Henry Breasted

A. P. Watt & Son (London), Doubleday Doran & Co. (New York), and Mrs. Georges Bambridge
for "Danny Deever" from Rudyard Kipling's *Barrack Room Ballads*

To the translators: John Wight for translations, hitherto unpublished, from Ennius and Horace; to Dr. Gardner Taplin likewise for translations from Horace; and also to Miss Jessie Degen for translations from the French; Dr. Karl W. Deutsch from the Czech, and Jeannette Eyre from the Russian. Thanks are also due to Professor E. K. Rand of Harvard for his kind suggestions with regard to the Latin translations.

The editors wish to thank their wives for their unfailing interest in and work on the book: to Hilda Rodman for her work in preparing the manuscript, to Elizabeth Eberhart for her interest over a period of three years in the project.

INDEX TO FIRST LINES

INDEX TO FIRST LINES

I burn for England with a living flame, 210
I hear and see not strips of cloth alone, 102
I know that I shall meet my fate, 130
I plucked a throstle from the throat of God, 211
I saw the vision of armies, 105
I watch them on the drill field, the awkward and the grave, 204
If I were to tell of our labours, our hard lodging, 19
If you could see, fair brother, how dead beat, 62
In the new city of marble and bright stone, 160
In the cold October night-time, when the wind raved round the land, 111
It seemed that out of battle I escaped, 152
It stops the town we come through. Workers raise, 188
It was by these men's valor that wide-lawned Tegea never burned, 28

Know this, 168
Krishna, Krishna, 38

Let the youth hardened by a sharp soldier's life, 36
Like a shower of rain, 30
lis-ten, 155
Lucky like Cook to travel and return, 203

Main artery of fighting, 137
Mother of God, whose burly love, 206
My brother Cain, the wounded, liked to sit, 195
My liege, I did deny no prisoners, 63
My soul looked down from a vague height with Death, 150
My soul stands at the window of my room, 187
my sweet old etcetera, 153
My triumph lasted till the drums, 107

Never until the mankind making, 200
next to of course god america i, 154
Night and the distant rumbling; for the train, 135
Noble is he who falls in front of battle, 12
Not a drum was heard, not a funeral note, 91
Not as you had dreamed was the battle's issue, 131
Not from the glory of the cloud's pile and rift, 197
Now entertain conjecture of a time, 66
Now the long blade of the sun, lying, 21

O Phoebus embattling the high wall of Ilium, 23
O sorrowful and ancient days, 45
O Strassburg, O Strassburg, 73
'Oh Polly love, Oh Polly, the rout has now begun, 86
Old battle field, fresh with Spring flowers again, 74
On Linden when the sun was low, 84
On this my sick-bed beats the world, 156
Once as we were sitting by, 196
Once more into the breach, dear friends, once more, 65
One morning in Spring, 203

[238]

One morning the world woke up and there was no news, 170
Our children's children will marvel, 147
Out of a fired ship, which, by no way, 69

Pergamon city of the Phrygians, 24
Pile the bodies high at Austerlitz and Waterloo, 136.
Pompeius, best of all my comrades, you and I, 34
Prepare, prepare the iron helm of War, 79

Rang'd on the line opposed, Antonius brings, 33
Ready they make hauberks Sarrazinese, 58
Red lips are not so red, 149

Say not the struggle naught availeth, 97
So they carried the dead man out of the fighting, 8
Sombre the night is, 146
Splendid burns the huge house with bronze; rich is the ample roof, 14
Still falls the rain, 165
Stone, bronze, stone, steel, stone, oakleaves, horses' heels, 144
Strengthened to live, strengthened to die for medals, 162
Success is counted sweetest, 108

Tell them in Lacedaemon, passerby, 15
That night your great guns unawares, 109
The Achaians have got Troy, upon this very day, 20
The balancing spaces are not disturbed, 186
The beauty of Israel is slain upon thy high places, 6
The bright moon lifts from the Mountain of Heaven, 45
The darkness crumbles away, 146
The first month of his absence, 201
The first shot was fired to Wagnerian music; 175
The gloomy hulls, in armour grim, 98
The glories of our blood and state, 71
The god of war, money changer of dead bodies, 17
The guns spell money's ultimate reason, 185
The landscape lies within my head, 211
The Lord is a man of war, 5
The mess is all asleep, my candle burns, 196
The morning of a cold month, 180
The mountain sheep are sweeter, 86
The naked earth is warm with spring, ·142
The prelude to this smooth scene—mark well! 112
Then they saw, 49
There was a sound of revelry by night, 88
There will be a rusty gun on the wall, sweetheart, 137
There you are once more near me, 138
Therefore Philippi saw once more the Roman battalions, 31
These fought in any case, 139
These, in the day when heaven was falling, 119
These set a crown of glory on their land, 14
They come, beset by riddling hail, 113

[239]

They fought last year by the upper valley of Son-Kan, 43
They fought south of the Castle, 30
They went forth to battle but they always fell, 134
They whose life is given utterly over to valor, 29
This is the Arsenal. From floor to ceiling, 95
This loneliness for you is like the wound, 209
Those stopped by the barrage, 171
Thou comest to me, thou exultest, seeing my beauty, 3
Through a green gorge the river like a fountain, 117
Thus much the fates have allotted me, and if, Maecenas, 37
Thus spoke Priam's shining son with words supplicating, 11

Vigil strange I kept on the field one night. 103

Walking next day upon the fatal shore, 70
We are those same children who amazed, 132
We grasp our battle spears: we don our breast-plates of hide, 28
We rode at a trot, 176
Well pleaseth me the sweet time of Easter, 62
'What are the bugles blowin' for?' said Files-on-Parade, 120
When our brother Fire was having his dog's day, 184
While going the road to sweet Athy, 128
Whilst the red spittle of the grape-shot sings, 118
Why do you lie with your legs ungainly huddled, 141
Why should vain Mortals tremble at the sight of, 82
Widely is flung, warning of slaughter, 55
Word over all, beautiful as the sky, 105

Yes, the coneys are scared by the thud of hoofs, 114
Yes. Why do we all, seeing of a soldier, bless him? 115
You are the millions, we are multitude, 124
You, I presume, could adroitly and gingerly, 25